THE BASKET BOOK

THE BASKET BOOK

By Lyn Siler

Watercolors and Illustrations
by Carolyn Kemp

A Sterling/**Lark** Book

 **Sterling Publishing Co., Inc.   New York**

Published in 1988 by Sterling Publishing Co., Inc.
387 Park Avenue South, New York, NY 10016

© 1988 Lyn Siler and Carolyn Kemp

A Sterling/Lark Book

Produced by Altamont Press
50 College Street, Asheville, NC 28801

Editor: Kate Mathews
Design: Rob Pulleyn and Thom Boswell
Production: Thom Boswell
Typesetting: Diane Deakin, Sandra Soto

Thanks, Lyn, for a wonderful experience.

Library of Congress Catalog Card Number: 87-51522

ISBN 0-8069-6828-1

Distributed in Canada by Oak Tree Press Company, Ltd.
c/o Canadian Manda Group, P.O. Box 920, Station U, Toronto, Ontario M8Z 5P9, Canada

Distributed in the United Kingdom by Blandford Press
Link House, West Street, Poole, Dorset BH15 1LL, England

Distributed in Australia by Capricorn Ltd.
P.O. Box 665, Lane Cove, New South Wales 2066, Australia

Printed in Hong Kong

For information on how you can have *Better Homes & Gardens*
magazine delivered to your door, write to:
Robert Austin, P.O. Box 4536, Des Moines, IA 50336.

I am grateful to many basketmakers, who have shared their talents and ideas with me, for their inspiration and guidance. Among those, I would especially like to thank:

Brenda Sutton of Danbury, N.C. . . . for giving me my first lesson in basketmaking,

Hazel Whittington of Horse Shoe, N.C. ... (a charter member of the Southern Highland Handicraft Guild) for "talking me through" my first few baskets,

Jim and Pat Laughridge of Salisbury, N.C. ... who are largely responsible for the "basketry renaissance" and who were among the first to make materials available to all of us,

Judy Wobbleton of Goldsboro, N.C. . . . for her *invaluable* assistance,

Shelby Underwood of Sanford, N.C. . . . for having such a wonderful, inspiring collection of baskets, so generously sharing them, and for being such a very special person,

and Carolyn Kemp of Matthews, N.C. ... who is so incredibly talented ... for making our paths cross again.

Lyn Siler
Goldsboro, North Carolina

*To all the basketmakers of yesteryear who so generously left us
heir to a wealth of basketmaking standards which we,
who love the craft, may strive to achieve.*

CONTENTS

Lyn Siler learned to make baskets while living in the mountains of western North Carolina. For eleven years prior to making and selling supplies for baskets full time, she was a high school English teacher. Born, raised, and educated in North Carolina, Lyn has traveled extensively to conduct seminars and workshops throughout the country. She is presently concentrating on the basketry of the Cherokee Indians.

Lyn is the author of a highly successful series of instructional books called *How to Make Baskets*, from which thousands have learned the craft.

Under her guidance, the North Carolina Basketmakers Association was founded in 1986. Lyn is also a member of the Association of Michigan Basketmakers, North Country Basketmakers Guild, and the Society of Craft Designers.

Carolyn Kemp was born in Salem, Massachusetts, grew up in Cincinnati, Ohio, and graduated from Miami University in Oxford, Ohio. Painting in San Francisco, she became one of the "Top Ten" artists at the (Union St.) San Francisco Artists Cooperative Gallery. She also served on their Board of Directors.

Living in Eden, North Carolina, she divides her time between family and her art work. Co-author of five books on basketmaking, she also paints and teaches watercolor workshops.

Her work is in the collection of Wachovia Bank, Miller Brewing Company, and numerous other companies and individuals.

OLD BASKETS

As every basketmaker knows,
Old baskets, like old friends
Just get a little grayer
And become more valuable
With the passing of time.

from Handling White Oak
by Jim Bennett

INTRODUCTION

This is a book about baskets — old ones and new ones. It is a study in watercolor of old baskets and an instructional tool for making reproductions of the baskets our forefathers made. Every attempt has been made to retain the authenticity of time-honored construction methods, whether duplicating an old basket or creating a new basket.

Your ancestors, no matter who or where they were, *did* make baskets. In every civilization and every part of the world, basketmaking has been practiced. Needed as carrying vessels, baskets were probably replaced by clay pots, the clay having been pressed around a basket for molding. If you wonder about the materials your forefathers used for their baskets, simply learn what kind of trees, bushes, vines, or grasses grew where they lived and you'll have your answer.

Baskets have been made from any wood, vine, leaf, or fiber that could be formed into a desirable shape. Not only did early basketmakers use the materials that were available, they also used the styles and techniques their ancestors (or even they, themselves) had used in the "old country." Our well-known Egg, Potato, Melon, and other gathering baskets are direct descendants of Irish, Welsh, Scottish, or English baskets, although not necessarily called by the same names.

As anyone who frequents antique shops knows, the price of an old basket can be very dear. A renewed interest in our past and a desire for things that at least "look" old have brought about something of a renaissance in basketmaking in recent years, with basketmakers everywhere reproducing whatever style baskets they happen to prefer.

Rattan core, known to most of us as reed, has been used in this country to some extent for many years. But the increasing number of new basketmakers, coupled with the scarcity of native woods, has meant that larger quantities of supplies must be imported to replace many of the natural materials that were once used. Flat reed has replaced oak, ash, and hickory splints. Round reed has replaced oak, willow, and other vine-like materials that were used for ribbed or twined baskets; it has even replaced natural materials that once served as the "core" of coiled baskets. So, the kind or size reed chosen today depends upon the type of basket to be reproduced.

There is always some controversy about the origins of the names of baskets. In times past, baskets were usually named for their uses, the areas in which they were made, the people who made them, or occasionally objects that the baskets resembled. The Shaker Cat-Head, for instance, is so called because the basket resembles a cat's head when it is held upside down, and because it was made in Shaker communities. Although a square "market-type" basket called a Kentucky Egg Basket can be found, the most universally known egg basket is the "flat-" or "twin-bottomed" basket

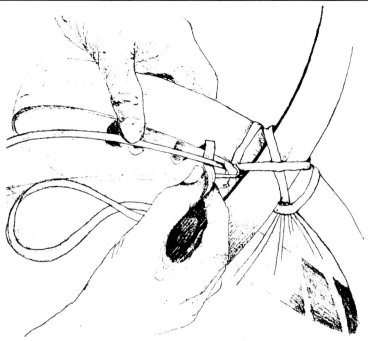

associated with the mountain areas of the southeastern United States. It was probably used for gathering eggs because the eggs didn't roll in the gizzard-shaped bottom. Evidently, more people gathered potatoes in a round, side-handled basket than any other; hence, the potato basket. Sometime along the way, someone realized that a shallow basket with a tall handle was perfect for gathering flowers, so today we have a flower or provender basket. The oriole basket only looks like an oriole's nest — it's not meant for birds. When it comes to basket names, either a particular name "caught on" and lasted through the ages or it didn't, and was called something different by everyone who used it.

An interesting fact about the age-old craft of basketmaking is that, while many other crafts have become mechanized, no one has ever invented a machine that can make baskets. They are still handmade, even in Taiwan. It's not even an easy task to mass-produce baskets with the aid of molds, electric saws and sanders, and a multitude of "assembly line" processes. In fact, no one has ever improved upon the earliest and most basic techniques of basketmaking.

Today's basketmakers range from the purist, who still fells the trees to make traditional utilitarian baskets, to the artist-basketmaker, whose interest is primarily aesthetic and who uses any and every material imaginable. Typically, beginning basketmakers experiment with many techniques and eventually settle on one or two preferred styles or methods.

Whether your style happens to lean to the traditional or the outrageous, there are so many interesting variations to be tested that you shouldn't rule out anything. Don't be afraid to experiment — some of my best efforts have been the results of experimentation. And, above all, remember that there are no "bad" baskets. If your basket isn't just like another's, yours is simply blessed with personality. Your imagination is your only limitation.

My dearest old friend
was a worker of wood ...
of the finest kind
until the day she died.

She learned to make baskets from her mother,
as naturally as she had learned to walk,
and it never occurred to her
that she was a master of her craft or an artist.
She created ... usually out of necessity,
and if you had told her she was "talented" or "gifted,"
she would have had a good hearty laugh.

When I was very young,
I sat on the giant, grey boulder
and watched her swift, skilled fingers
pull the weavers through the ribs
and wished she would teach me.
I was too young, she said.

Later, I helped her ...
whether she wanted me or not ...
gather wisteria, honeysuckle, willow, grasses ...
and sometimes she even let me follow her into the woods
(on the north side of the mountain, of course)
to find a white oak tree to split.
Not just any oak, mind you, just the right one.
Young, straight, and tall.
One that had reached very straight ... looking for the sun.
And then we "busted it," right down the middle.
"Got to be cut with the grain," she always said.
And with the first blow of the axe,
the too-sweet smell of fresh cut wood engulfed us.
The thought came to me once that the strange aroma
gave her some wonderful magic ... a supernatural energy.
She would breathe in long and slow, as if to fill herself
with all of it she could hold.

I've watched lots of folks split wood,
but none of them seemed to love it like she did.
She pulled the splits gently but firmly
like the stern but loving mother ...
guiding the grain with her seasoned touch.
And often she rubbed them across her cheek in what seemed
a test of their smoothness.
Or maybe it was just a gesture of love.

Word of Hannah's skills spread
and her house became a stopping place for many.
Some came to place their orders.
Some came to admire and others came just to "talk baskets."
Since she rarely traveled, she always welcomed new friends.
Sharing her craft was one of her greatest joys and it completed
the cycle ... from conception, through preparation and construction...

TERMINOLOGY

aging: the process that occurs when a basket turns dark from natural environmental elements.

ash splints: strips of ash that are thinned enough to use for stakes or weavers.

awl: a tool resembling an ice pick used for opening spaces and making holes in reed. It is shorter and not as sharply pointed as an ice pick.

base: the bottom of a basket; woven mat.

bevel: to cut a square edge to a sloping edge; scarf.

bow-knot ear: a four-point lashing ear, wrapped only one time and "tied" in front.

braided God's Eye: a four-point lashing like the regular God's Eye except it is interwoven and appears braided to the eye; woven God's Eye.

braided handle: any of several different methods of interweaving the reed around the handle. Specifically: the wheat braid.

brake: a short piece of reed woven alternately above the beginning of a weaver to hold it in place.

butt: to bring the ends of any two pieces together, flush against each other.

cane: the outer peel of rattan, used in weaving as an embellishment and on chair bottoms.

coil: reed wound and tied in a circle.

coiling: a weaving technique using an inner core which is wrapped solidly with a smaller thread.

chase weave: a method of weaving with two weavers at once. Continuous weaving over an even number of stakes. The weaver moves first, and the chaser (the other weaver) follows alternately.

continuous weave: weaving done over an odd number of stakes. It is not done one row at a time, but rather continuously from beginning to end, adding weavers periodically.

"D" handle: a basket handle that continues across the bottom of the basket and turned on its side resembles the letter "D."

diagonal weave: a method of weaving in which the elements interweave with themselves. Also called diagonal plaiting and oblique weaving.

double-bottom: a method of construction in which one base is woven and a second (woven) one is placed on top of the first.

dyeing: coloring reed with any number of natural or commercial dyes.

ear: (1) weaving or lashing done at the intersecting point of the rim and handle that holds the two pieces securely. (2) lashing into which the ribs are inserted. (3) loops that join a "swing" handle to the basket.

embellishment: any decorative treatment done to the handle or body of the basket, nonessential to its construction.

fanny: the twin, gizzard-shaped bottom of an Egg basket; buttocks.

filling in: on some ribbed baskets a wedge-shaped area remains unwoven when the rim is full; it must be filled in by some type of "back and forth" weaving; also called "packing."

five-point lashing: a lashing (ear) done around any five intersecting pieces.

frame: the support (usually wood) around which the basket is woven.

French slewing: a strong diagonal randing pattern that uses short rods (weavers) that are begun at the base one at a time.

God's Eye: a four-point lashing; ear.

grapevine: a vine used for weaving baskets and handles.

hairs: the splinters from the reed that usually occur from overuse, to be clipped or singed when the basket is finished.

handle: the part of the basket by which it is carried.

honeysuckle: a wild vine used for weaving baskets, smaller than grapevine.

hoop: ring or piece of wood shaped into a circle; machine or handmade, present in ribbed baskets.

lasher: the piece of reed that wraps around and secures all the rim pieces together.

lashing: the act of wrapping all the rim pieces or wrapping the ear; the pieces of reed used to wrap are also referred to as "lashing."

loop: an ear that holds the swing handle and pushes down into the basket.

losing a lasher: a means of hiding the end of the reed in the rim or in the weaving.

mat: the woven base of a flat basket.

notch: the indented space on a push-in handle made to fit under the rim and prevent the handle from pulling out.

oak splints: strips of oak wood thinned enough to use as stakes or weavers; also called "splits."

oblique weave: diagonal plaiting or weaving.

osier: any of various willows that have tough, flexible twigs or branches which are used for wickerwork.

plaited: woven.

pre-form: shaped or formed before being used.

randing: a simple over-under weaving with a single weaver and an odd number of stakes.

rattan: a climbing palm (vine) from which reed is made.

reed: the inner core of rattan that has been cut into flat, round, flat oval, half round, or oval shapes; used for baskets and furniture.

rib: the round or oval pieces that extend from one side of the basket to the other and form the basic skeleton.

rim: the pieces, inside and outside, that fit over the top row of weaving to form an edge and give stability to the sides.

rim filler: a piece of round reed, seagrass, or other suitable material that goes between and on top of the two rim pieces.

scarf: a joint in which the ends of any two pieces are cut so they overlap each other and join firmly.

scarfing: to join by cutting the two end pieces, usually beveled or on a slant, so they fit together smoothly.

shaper: an instrument used for shaving away wood; a small rasp.

sight: to "look at" a basket frame and determine the rib lengths to give the desired shape; to "eyeball."

slewing: a wickerwork weave done with two or more paired weavers in a randing pattern.

spiral: (1) the result of twill weaving (under two, over two) continuously over an odd number of spokes. (2) a gradually widening curve winding away from a base to create a design.

spline: a wedge-shaped reed made primarily for use with pressed cane; also used to make loops and handles in baskets.

splice: the place where two pieces of wood, having been scarfed, overlap.

spoke: the same as a stake, but laid circularly as spokes in a wheel.

staining: a term that has come to mean coloring reed to give it an aged look.

stake: pieces of the woven mat (base) which are upsett and become the upright elements.

stepping up: a term used in twill weaving meaning to start the next row one stake to the right (or left, as the case may be) of the starting point on the previous row.

swing handle: a handle attached to a basket by means of a loop or protruding ear that allows it to swing freely from side to side.

three-point lashing: the wrapping used to cover the intersecting point of any three elements.

three rod wale: when three weavers are inserted, each behind three consecutive stakes, with all three weaving, one at a time, over two-under one.

true: to measure the woven base making sure all sides are the correct length, adjusting if necessary, and marking corners.

tucking in: when the basket is woven, the outside stakes are pointed, bent over, and tucked into the weaving on the inside of the basket; also called "down staking."

twill: a method of weaving in which the weaver passes over and under the stakes, two at a time.

twining: a method of weaving (usually with round reed) using two or more elements that twist around each other as they weave around the spokes or stakes; also called "pairing."

two-point lashing: a wrapping used at the intersecting point of any two pieces.

upsett or upstake: to bend the stakes up and over upon themselves (toward the base) creating a crease at the base of the stake.

weaver: the fiber, often reed, used as the "weft" that moves over and under the stakes, spokes, or ribs (warp).

wicker: from the Swedish, *vikker*, meaning "willow" or "osier." Generally refers to any round, shoot-like material used for basketmaking.

wickerwork: a basketry technique that employs round, vertical stakes or spokes, and round weavers which are woven perpendicularly to the spokes.

willow: an osier which yields its long, slender branches for use in basket weaving.

wisteria: a climbing vine that is particularly flexible and used for basket weaving and for making basket handles.

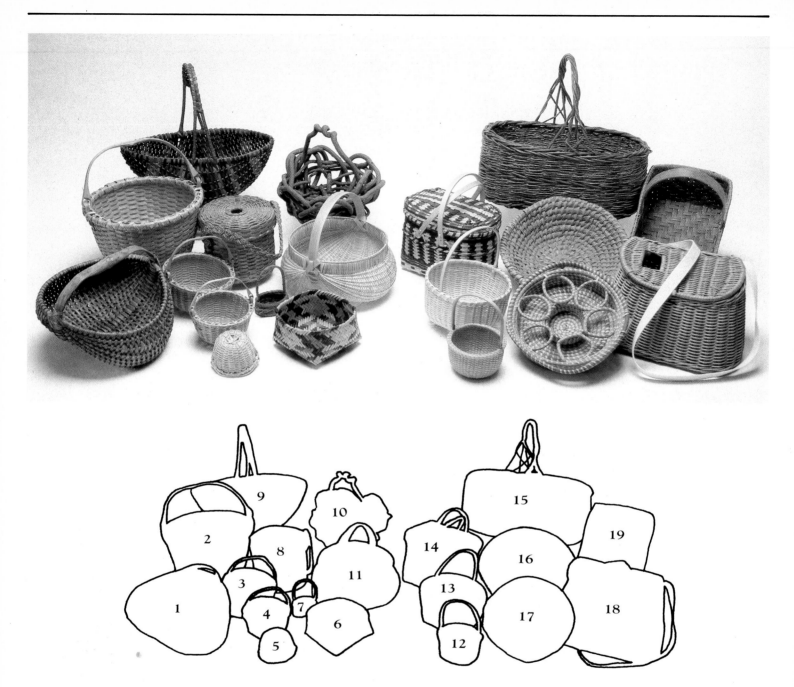

1. EGG BASKET (reed) with Dogwood Frame; made by Bob Whitley
2.-5. SWEETSTER BASKETS (brown ash); made by William & Lynn Thorpe
6. CHEROKEE DOUBLE WEAVE (river cane); made by Rowena Bradley
7. COILED TRINKET BASKET (pine needles); collection of Shelby Underwood
8. KNITTING BASKET (brown ash & sweetgrass); collection of Lyn Siler
9. GATHERING BASKET (white oak); collection of Lyn Siler
10. FREE FORM MELON BASKET (wisteria); collection of Carolyn Kemp
11. EGG BASKET (white oak); made by Ken & Kathleen Dalton

12. NANTUCKET LIGHTSHIP BASKET; made by Lyn Siler
13. SHAKER CAT-HEAD BASKET (brown ash); made by Heidi Frazier
14. CHEROKEE PURSE (white oak); made by Bessie Long
15. MARKET BASKET (willow); made by Mark Katz
16. COILED BREAD BASKET (Pennsylvania rye straw); collection of Shelby Underwood
17. COILED BEVERAGE TRAY (Charleston sweet grass); collection of Lyn Siler
18. FISHING CREEL (round reed); collection of Carolyn Kemp
19. TWILL WEAVE MARKET BASKET (reed); made by Carolyn Kemp

TOOLS

The tools and supplies needed for basketmaking are simple, inexpensive, and readily available. Most of the items shown here can be found in any household.

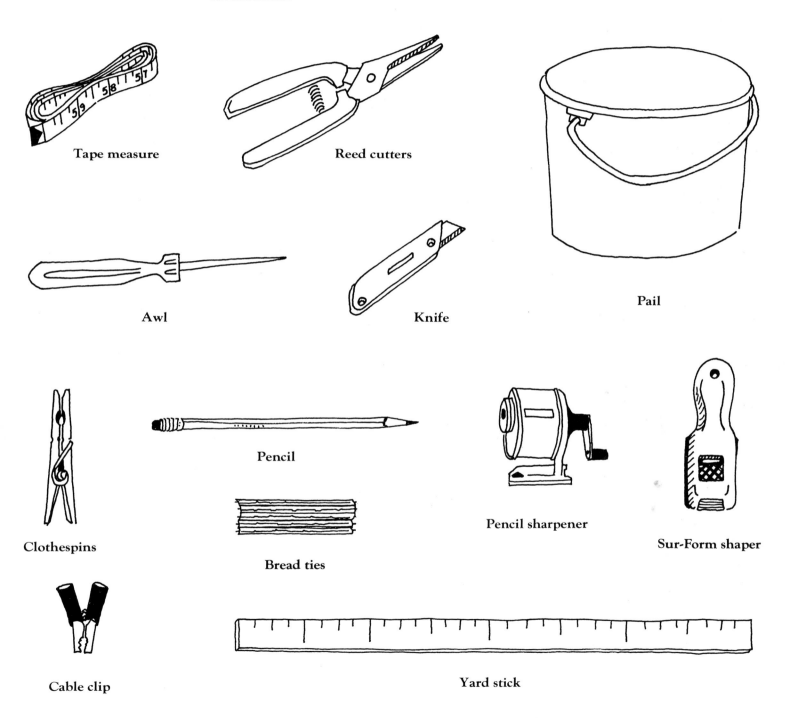

Tape measure

Reed cutters

Pail

Awl

Knife

Clothespins

Pencil

Pencil sharpener

Sur-Form shaper

Bread ties

Cable clip

Yard stick

MATERIALS

The most commonly used basketry reeds and grasses are shown here. All are available in a range of sizes and are packaged in manageable hanks, coils, or rolls. Basketry supplies can be found in craft and hobby stores, most weaving supply stores, and from mail order suppliers who advertise in craft and home decorating magazines.

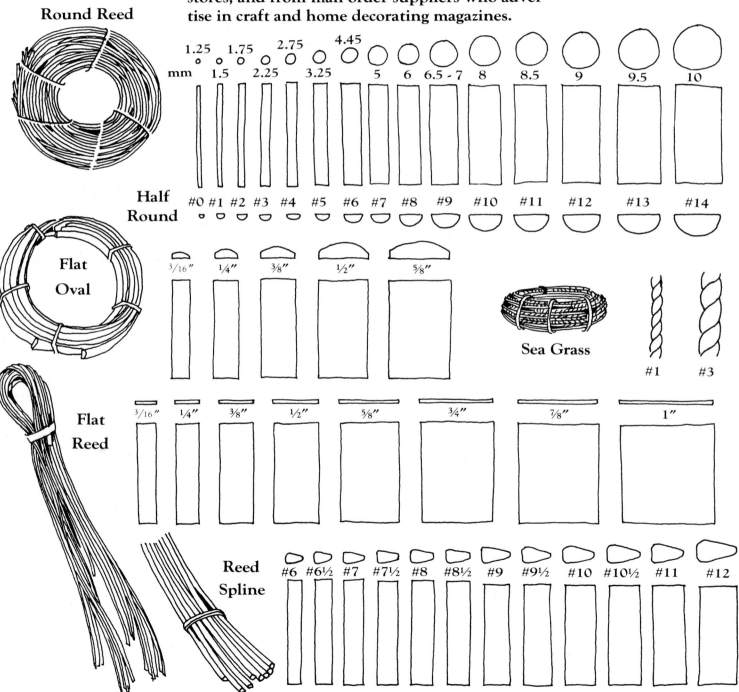

Round Reed

mm: 1.25 1.5 1.75 2.25 2.75 3.25 4.45 5 6 6.5 - 7 8 8.5 9 9.5 10

#0 #1 #2 #3 #4 #5 #6 #7 #8 #9 #10 #11 #12 #13 #14

Half Round

Flat Oval

3/16″ 1/4″ 3/8″ 1/2″ 5/8″

Sea Grass

#1 #3

Flat Reed

3/16″ 1/4″ 3/8″ 1/2″ 5/8″ 3/4″ 7/8″ 1″

Reed Spline

#6 #6½ #7 #7½ #8 #8½ #9 #9½ #10 #10½ #11 #12

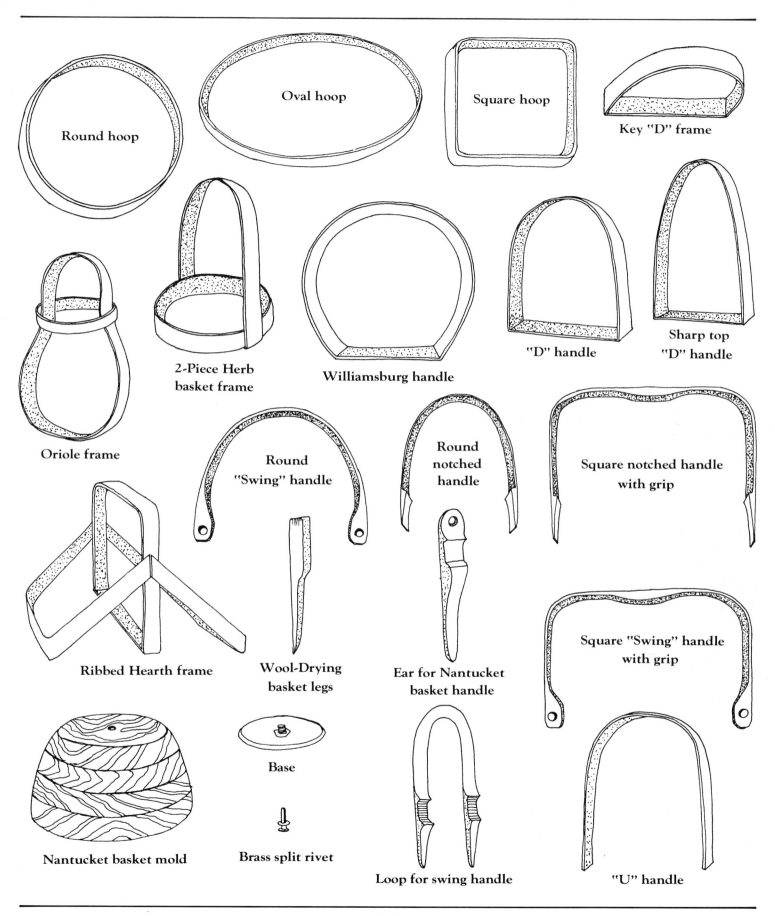

Round hoop

Oval hoop

Square hoop

Key "D" frame

Oriole frame

2-Piece Herb basket frame

Williamsburg handle

"D" handle

Sharp top "D" handle

Ribbed Hearth frame

Round "Swing" handle

Round notched handle

Square notched handle with grip

Wool-Drying basket legs

Ear for Nantucket basket handle

Square "Swing" handle with grip

Nantucket basket mold

Base

Brass split rivet

Loop for swing handle

"U" handle

EAR VARIATIONS

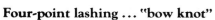

All ribbed baskets have some sort of lashing (called the "ear") that is used primarily to cover the intersecting points of the frame and indeed, secure the frame pieces in place. The following chart illustrates some of the possibilities of ears ... three-, four-, and five-point lashings.

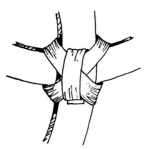

Four-point lashing ... "bow knot"

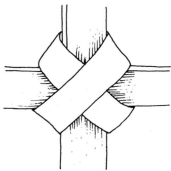

Four-point lashing ... "X"

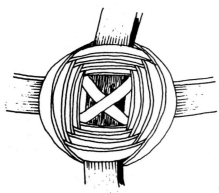

Four-point "round" lashing with "X"

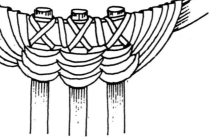

Four-point lashing ... "braided or woven God's Eye"

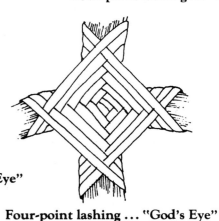

Four-point lashing ... "God's Eye"

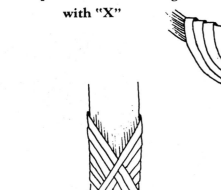

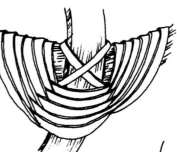

Three-point lashing with "X"

Four-point lashing ... "God's Eye"

Five-point lashing

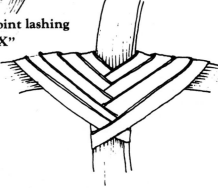

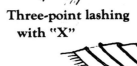

Five-point lashing with "X"

Three-point lashing without "X"

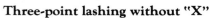

BASKET WEAVE VARIATIONS

There remains some controversy and confusion about the terminology used for methods of basketmaking. It is a matter of semantics, it seems, as most of us recognize a process when it is illustrated or demonstrated, by whatever term we use for that process.

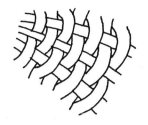

Plain weave

The following are methods of construction used in this book:

plain weave: weaving done with rigid stakes or spokes and "weavers" which wrap around the stakes in an "over one-under one" pattern. Variations are achieved by changing the number of "overs" and "unders."

plaiting: executed with two like or similar elements, either vertically, horizontally, or diagonally.

diagonal plaiting: a method of weaving with two like elements interwoven at right angles.

twining: a method used in wickerwork (for our purposes, with round reed) with two pieces "twisted" around a rigid spoke.

continuous weave: use of one weaver woven over an odd number of spokes.

chase-weave: use of two weavers (or one folded in half, producing two ends) over an even number of spokes.

twill weaving: a method of weaving with an even number of stakes and the weaver passing over two and under two stakes at a time.

three-rod wale: a method of wickerwork with any number of rigid spokes and three weavers, each weaving over two and behind one.

randing: another term for weaving, usually referring to round reed or willow. It is a simple over and under weave, done with an even number of stakes.

coiling: an extremely tight and rigid method of basket construction executed by using a rigid core that is wrapped and stitched with a softer, more flexible material. Rows of the wrapped core are stacked (coiled) rather than woven.

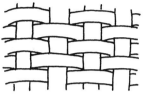

Plaiting

Diagonal plaiting

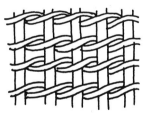

Twining

Continuous weave

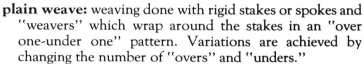

Chase-weave

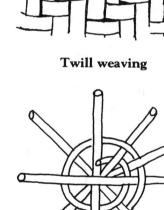

Twill weaving

Randing

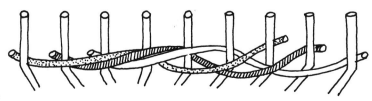

Three-rod wale

Coiling

RIBBED BASKET VARIATIONS

Ribbed baskets are all constructed by the same basic technique. The elements required are: a frame (a hoop or hoops), ribs, and weavers. Probably the best known ribbed basket is recognized as the Egg Basket. All one need do to create another kind of ribbed basket is vary the rib lengths and hoop sizes. The following chart demonstrates only a few variations achieved by varying hoop and rib dimensions as well as "decorative trim" and "ear" lashings.

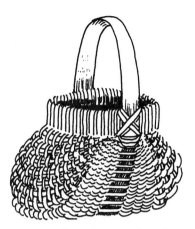

Very deep Egg or Oriole basket with "X" ear

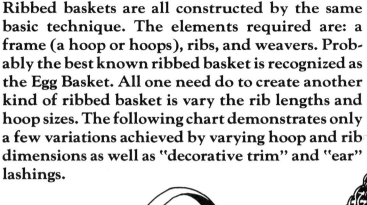

Flat bottom Egg with braided God's Eye and rim lip.

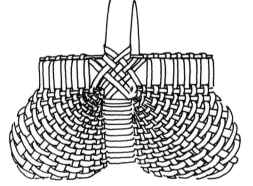

Twin bottom Egg with braided ear (braided God's Eye)

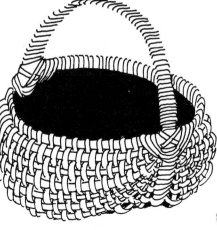

Flat bottom Egg with three-point lashing ear

Double handle Egg with five-point lashing ear

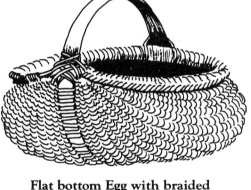

Melon basket with four-point lashed round ear

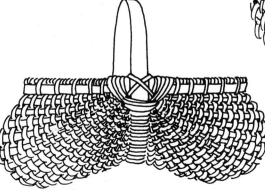

Oval Egg with three-point lashing ear and wrapped rim rib

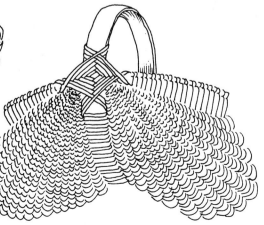

Very full-fannied Egg with four-point lashing (God's Eye)

HELPFUL HINTS

How To Measure Your Own Rib Lengths

If you are going to be a basketmaker, you must learn to create your own rib lengths. Your forefathers didn't have any measurements; they "eyeballed" them, which is exactly what you must learn to do. Granted, it takes some practice, but you can do it if you want to. Here's how:

- Get a mental picture of the shape you want, visualizing the size of the hoops, the height of the handle, the depth of the basket, and other details. Sketch it on paper and refer to the sketch often.
- Join hoops and construct ears.
- Sharpen one end of a piece of reed (the size you think you need) and push the sharpened end into the ear. Then hold the piece around to the other ear, allowing it to protrude to the correct fullness. Allow about ½" to be pushed into the other ear, mark and cut. Sharpen the other end.
- Cut another rib for the other side, just like the first one. Repeat this procedure for each rib. Really *look* at your basket, and make adjustments if the shape isn't looking like you want it to. Stand away from it so you can study it objectively; sometimes we're too close to really see the shape. See **Diagram 1**.

How To Measure Your Own Staked Baskets

This is a simple mathematical process. Determine the size basket you want; for example, let's make a 10" wide by 16" long by 6" deep basket. To get a length measurement, add the base length (16") and each side depth (6" on each side or 12"), and then add 6" (3" on each side) to tuck in at the top: 16" + 12" (2 sides) + 6" (tucking) = 34".

To get the width measurement, add the base width (10") and each side depth (6") with the same 6" for tucking: 10" + 12" (two sides) + 6" = 28".

The only thing left to determine is what size reed to use, and therefore, how many of each to cut. Draw off the area and use a ruler to figure out how many pieces of each to use. Don't forget to add spaces between stakes. See **Diagram 2**.

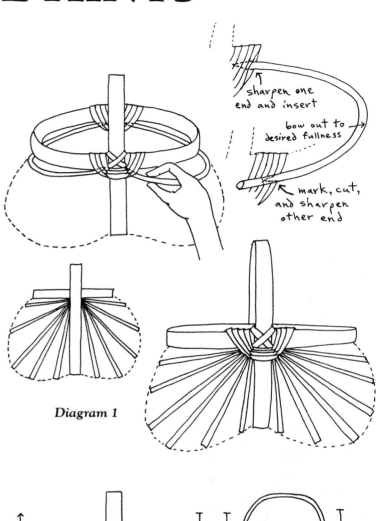

sharpen one end and insert

bow out to desired fullness

mark, cut, and sharpen other end

Diagram 1

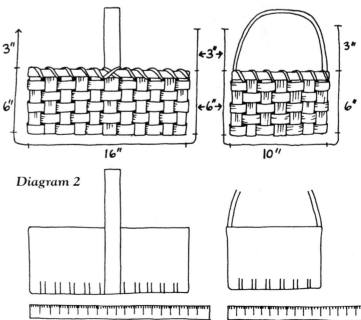

Diagram 2

How To Measure Spokes For A Round Basket

Simple! Determine the diameter of the base, 8″ in this case. Add to that the height you want, 4″ in this case, and then add the 6″ for tucking in: 8″ + 8″ (4″ for each side) + 6″ = 22″. How many stakes to be cut will be determined by the size reed you use and how close together you want the spokes. You can use more stakes and start weaving closer in to the center if you taper the center as in the drawing. See *Diagram 3*.

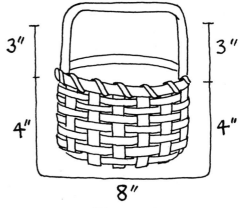

Diagram 3

How To Identify The Wrong Side Of Reed

There are exceptional cases in which you can hardly identify a wrong and right side of reed, but normally when it is bent over your finger, the wrong side "splinters" and looks very "hairy" while the right side remains smooth. See *Diagram 4*.

Where To Start Weaving On A Staked Or Spoked Basket

Always begin the first row by wrapping the weaver around the stake that originates from underneath the woven mat or base. These stakes are anchored by a horizontal stake; the top ones are not and will not stay in place if you begin weaving around them. If you have twined around the base of a basket, this doesn't apply because all the stakes are anchored. See *Diagram 5*.

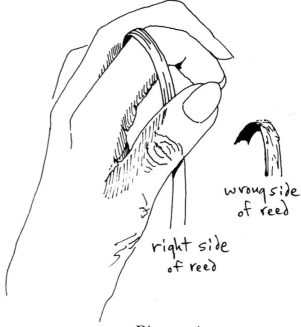

wrong side of reed

right side of reed

Diagram 4

Where To Start Weaving On An Even Staked Basket

To avoid creating a build-up from repeatedly starting and stopping (and consequently overlapping) in the same spot, move the basket a quarter turn after every row. That way you won't have to search for the ending on the last row and will know right away where to begin the next.

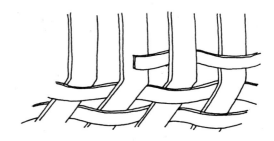

Diagram 5

How To End A Row When Weaving Individual Rows

If you start the weaver on the outside of the basket (it is easier to see what is happening that way), weave all the way around, then continue weaving over the starting point and on to the fourth stake. Cut the weaver so its end lies in the middle of the fourth stake. Even though it doesn't appear to be hidden now, it will be when, on the next row, that stake stands. See *Diagram 6*.

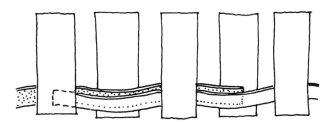

Diagram 6

Losing A Lasher

To "lose a lasher" means to put it somewhere it can't be seen. Usually, the best way is to push it up between the two rim pieces, over the woven basket side, and back down on the other side. Cut it flush with the rim edge and it will never be seen.

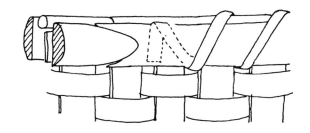

Diagram 7

Where To Begin Lashing The Rim

If you place your splices on each rim (inner and outer) *near* (not at the same spot, but near) the joint of the rim filler, and begin lashing just past all those "joints," any fullness you might have in the rim pieces will be "worked out" at the end. See *Diagram 7*.

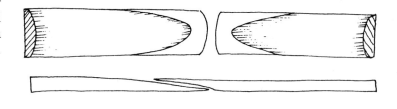

Scarfing Or Beveling The Ends Of Rim Pieces

Anyone can see that two pieces of flat oval overlaid are going to be thicker than the rest of the reed. If some of the oval side is shaved away and the two overlapped areas are "scarfed" to fit together, you should have a joint the same thickness as the rest of the rim. This is one of the small details that contribute to a well-made basket. See *Diagram 8*.

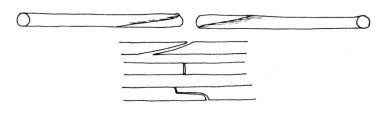

Diagram 8

How To Put A Handle On A Basket

Always put the handle on the outside of the rim. Think about it — if the handle hoop is on the inside of the rim hoop, it can move, but where can it go if it is on the outside? See *Diagram 9*.

How To Add On A Weaver Or Change Colors In A God's Eye

If a weaver breaks or runs out, the best way to add another is to have it end on a diagonal (in *Diagram 10*, it is ending at 4). Go back and start a new one by slipping the end under the old weaver and weave over the old one behind 3, then continue as usual.

If your God's Eye began with a wrap around 1, to make a complete revolution, it must return to 1. To change colors, stop the weaver at 1; tuck a new end into the wraps *behind* 1, bringing it around and over the new end, then continue as usual. See *Diagram 10*.

Shaping And Reshaping

In case your shaping doesn't quite work out while you are weaving the basket, it almost always can be reshaped. Rewet the basket, being very careful not to soak any machine-made hoops, and mold with your hands to reshape. If the basket does not sit level, place a heavy object on the side that isn't sitting properly and let it dry into shape. Bricks, stones, soup cans, or other heavy objects can serve as weights. See *Diagram 11*.

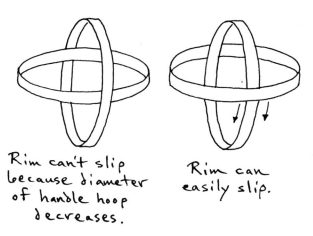

Rim can't slip because diameter of handle hoop decreases.

Rim can easily slip.

Diagram 9

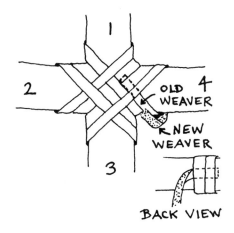

Diagram 10

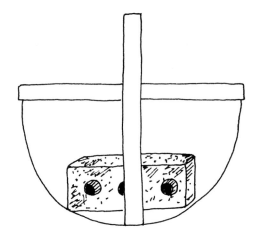

Diagram 11

Twilling

Twill weaving is a matter of the warp passing over two or more elements of the weft. When you are taking the weaver over two stakes, "stepping up" means to weave over the second stake that was covered on the row before plus the next one that was not covered before. "Dropping back" is to weave over a new, uncovered stake and the first of the two that were covered the last row. See **Diagrams 12A** and **12B**.

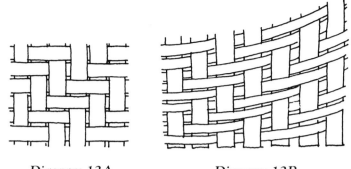

Diagram 12A   *Diagram 12B*

Counting Rows

- On a God's Eye, count rows accurately only from the back.
- On a regular 3-point lashing, count from the rim.
- On a ribbed basket, count actual rows, not from the rim. See **Diagram 13**.

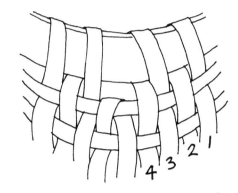

Diagram 13

Truing A Base

To true a base means to measure it on all sides and adjust anything that is not correct. When it is adjusted and you are sure the measurements are correct, mark the corners in pencil on the two adjacent sides. When you begin weaving, you will be aware of any shifting because the corner marks will be out of alignment. See **Diagram 14**.

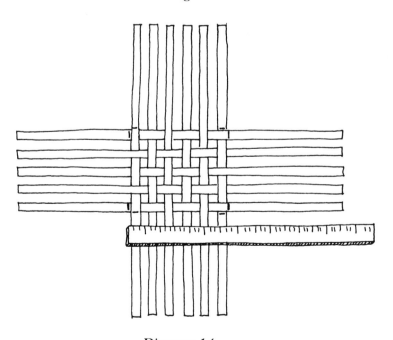

Diagram 14

Sharpening Ribs

An electric pencil sharpener usually works; a hand-turned one works better. Even the little hand-held school sharpener will work, but a sharp knife works best. None of the sharpeners I have seen give a long enough tapered end. Sometimes, depending on where you are inserting ribs, you will need to begin tapering as far as 1½″ - 2″ from the end. See *Diagram 15*.

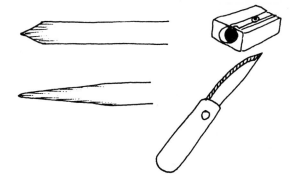

Diagram 15

How To Replace A Broken Stake

If a stake breaks (or is too short), simply cut a length of reed similar in size and slide it into the weaving on top of the broken stake down to the base of the basket. The new piece should be exposed to the outside of the basket. See *Diagram 16*.

How To Replace A Broken Spoke

Use the same procedure as with the broken stake.

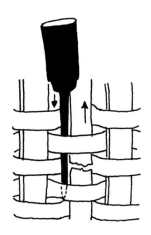

Diagram 16

How To Replace A Broken Rib

- Remove the broken rib by pulling one piece out and then the other.
- Insert an awl into the weaving to hold the weavers in place until you replace the rib.
- Cut another rib of equal size and length; soak it until it is *very* flexible.
- Bend the rib severely enough so that both ends can be started into the weaving at once.
- Gradually work the two ends of the new rib into the weaving while allowing the new rib to form itself to the curve of the original rib. See *Diagram 17*.

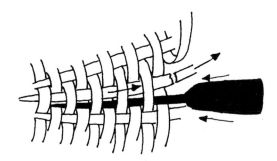

Diagram 17

How To Make Down Staking Easier

On some baskets, down staking (or tucking the tops of the outside stakes to the inside) is more difficult than on others. The closer the stakes are to each other and the tighter the weaving, the harder it is to get the stake to tuck in. If you trim part of the stake away (some from each side), you are left with a slender piece of reed to push into the weaving — much easier and just as effective. See *Diagram 18.*

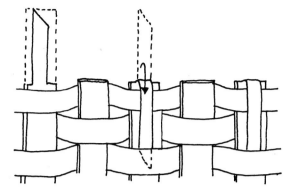

Diagram 18

Using A "Brake" Instead Of Clothespins

Just in case you should be caught without your clothespins, use a "brake" to hold the weavers in place while starting to weave. Cut a piece of the widest flat reed you have, long enough to weave around three or four stakes. It will hold the weaver in place; in fact, you may not even want to use clothespins again. See *Diagram 19.*

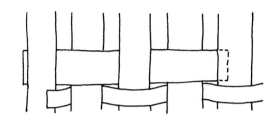

Diagram 19

Making Ears Or Lashings Tight

The tighter you can weave the ears, the better. One of the problems common to beginning basketmakers is keeping ribs in place while beginning to weave. This can be resolved by constructing the ears tighter, firmer, and with more tension. The reed to be inserted will loosen the ear, so you don't need to start out with it loose. See *Diagram 20.*

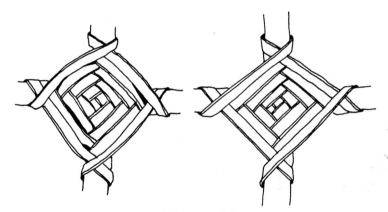

· *Diagram 20*

How To Fill In Unwoven Areas

There are some ribbed baskets in which some filling in will be necessary. For example, on a "full fanny" Egg basket or any ellipsoidal ribbed basket, the rims and bottom of the handle hoop will naturally fill with weavers more quickly than the other fuller parts of the basket, leaving an oval or wedge-shaped area to be filled in. *Diagrams 21A, B,* and **C** illustrate three different methods of accomplishing this. In *21A*, the weaver turns around the first available rib and reverses after it will no longer fit around the rim. In *21B*, the weaver is cut (when no more can be squeezed in at the rim) and a new weaver is added over an existing one. *Diagram 21C* shows weaving an oval area, growing to a point, and then decreasing by reversing directions at prescribed points.

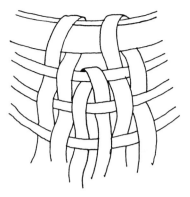

Diagram 21A

Repairing Old Baskets

There is no simple way to repair an old basket; brittleness caused by age is usually the most serious problem. If it has been painted, the first proces is to remove the paint, which may cause the material to become even more brittle. Experience has taught me to first attempt to restore some of the moisture to the wood. I do so by misting it often with a fine spray of water. Putting the basket in a bathroom where steam can penetrate it also helps to soften the wood so that it is more pliable and, therefore, easier to repair.

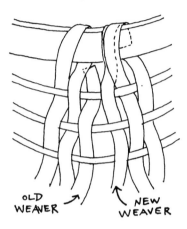

OLD WEAVER   NEW WEAVER

Diagram 21B

How To Avoid Loosely Woven Baskets

Because every basketmaker is anxious to see the product, it is easy to skip this step, but it is better if you can force yourself to let the basket dry once the sides are woven and before you add the rim. Any wood, and especially a porous one like reed, expands widthwise when wet and shrinks when dry. After it's dry, sometimes there is room for adding another row of weaving before putting on the rim.

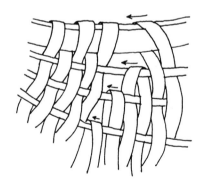

Diagram 21C

Quality Of Reed

There is "bad" reed — it shreds or splits when woven or is so brittle that it snaps at the slightest touch. A common complaint is that reed is too thick or too thin, but neither of these characteristics makes it "bad" reed. There are some baskets, like a market basket or large spoked basket, that need the strength of heavy or thick reed; others, like the small or medium egg basket, need the thinner and more flexible reed for weaving. Nearly every type of reed can be used for something.

How To Determine The Quality Of Baskets

This is like the question of whether an old basket is worth the selling price — the only answer is, "If you really want it, then it's worth the price." To some extent, the same goes for judging a basket's quality. I have seen many poorly constructed baskets find homes quite easily because the buyers didn't know what qualities to look for or because they simply liked the basket and didn't care about the quality. I suspect that if you asked 50 people what constitutes a "well-made" basket, you would get at least 40 different answers. These are my opinions:

- It is impossible for ribbed baskets to have too many ribs. The smaller the ribs, the tighter the weaving. The very best quality egg baskets are woven so tightly and have so many ribs, they will almost hold water.
- Flat-bottom round or square baskets should be tightly packed with no loose weavers and should display consistent weaving tension. They should also be constructed sturdily enough to hold any items you might want to carry in them.
- There is no reason that the ends of weavers ever need to show on the inside or the outside of a basket. With minimal effort, they can be adjusted behind a stake or behind the rest of the weaver.
- When overlapping the ends of the rim, the two pieces should be scarfed evenly enough that the area of overlap is no thicker than the rest of the rim.
- "Hairs" should be trimmed when the basket is finished.
- On any basket, the craftsmanship should never distract from the overall design.

How to Store Damp Weavers

You never want to oversoak weavers, so soak them for a short period and keep them in a towel or plastic bag while you weave. I often weave as I travel, so I take along damp weavers in a bag, which is fine for a few hours or even a day. In hot and humid conditions, however, damp weavers will mildew, so keep a close eye on them.

How To Dye Reed

There are several basketry dyes now on the market; all have printed how-to instructions. You can dye individual strips or many pieces coiled together, or dip the whole finished basket. (Note that machine-made hoops will come apart when soaked, as they are glued.)

If has been my experience that the best method of setting the dye is to use boiling (or almost boiling) water. I never leave reed in the dye to darken; I only dip. If I don't achieve the shade I want, I dip again, because soaking reed in very hot water tends to dry it, causing it to split and fray more easily when it is woven.

Opinions about dyeing and staining vary greatly — I recommend using natural or vegetable dyes. I believe that oil-based stains close the quickly penetrated pores of reed, therefore making it impossible to replace any moisture later on. None of the packaged basketry dyes are oil-based.

If you want an "aged" look for your basket, consider using a brown or grey dye or making your own stain from walnut, pecan, hickory, acorn, or almost any other hull. If you find you enjoy making your own dyes, try other natural sources like berries, leaves, or bark; there are many good books on the subject of natural dyeing. My recipe for making a walnut stain follows:

- Confine the hulls (you don't necessarily need to remove the nut) in something that will not deteriorate (I have found old pantyhose to be the perfect container — you will be amazed at how far a leg will stretch!). The acid in the walnut hulls will eat through materials that are not synthetic; fine mesh wire, nylon, or polyester work well.
- Put the hulls in a container — I use a 30-gallon galvanized garbage can, but you may want to use something smaller.
- Cover them with rain water or Calgon. Natural dyes work best with soft water but plain water is sufficient. Let the hulls sit, covered, for several days. If you want your stain immediately, you will need to boil the hulls.

METRIC CONVERSION
INCHES TO CENTIMETERS

INCHES	CM	INCHES	CM
⅛	0.3	19	48.3
¼	0.6	20	50.8
⅜	1.0	21	53.3
½	1.3	22	55.9
⅝	1.6	23	58.4
¾	1.9	24	61.0
⅞	2.2	25	63.5
1	2.5	26	66.0
1¼	3.2	27	68.6
1½	3.8	28	71.1
1¾	4.4	29	73.7
2	5.1	30	76.2
2½	6.4	31	78.7
3	7.6	32	81.3
3½	8.9	33	83.8
4	10.2	34	86.4
4½	11.4	35	88.9
5	12.7	36	91.4
6	15.2	37	94.0
7	17.8	38	96.5
8	20.3	39	99.1
9	22.9	40	101.6
10	25.4	41	104.1
11	27.9	42	106.7
12	30.5	43	109.2
13	33.0	44	111.8
14	35.6	45	114.3
15	38.1	46	116.8
16	40.6	47	119.4
17	43.2	48	121.9
18	45.7	49	124.5
		50	127.0

1. SERVICE BASKETS

... In the days before paper bags and stainless steel,
people needed carrying containers,
so Hannah made good, strong service baskets.
They were used to haul vegetables from the garden,
take to market, or hold freshly gathered eggs or flowers.

They were made with ribs ...
They were round ...   Square ...   Oval ...

AMY'S BASKET

Like all other baskets in this book, Amy's basket is not new. I studied a very old one, a family heirloom, in the North Carolina mountains. It was quite worn and well-used. My daughter commented that it had more character than any basket she had ever seen and that we should reproduce it. Hence, "Amy's Basket."

Finished Size

8" x 8" x 12"

Materials

8" x 12" sharp top "D" handle
¾" flat reed (stakes)
3/16" or ¼" flat oval reed (weavers)
⅜" flat reed (weavers)
¼" flat reed (lashing)
#6 round reed (rim filler)
⅝" flat oval reed (rim)

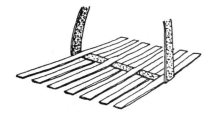

Diagram 1

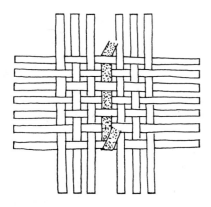

Diagram 2

The "D" handle is specially made to decrease in width from the bottom to the top, as do the sides of the basket. The handle will give you a guide by which to shape the sides. Use the measurements here as a guide, but by all means experiment with your own measurements and materials. Create your own heirloom. A regular "D" handle can be used. You simply must control the shape by pulling tightly on the weaver as you proceed up the sides, thereby forming the handle to the shape you desire.

Preparing The Materials And Weaving The Bottom

From the ¾" flat reed, cut 13 pieces 30" long. With a pencil, mark the center of all the pieces on the wrong (rough) side. Also, mark the halfway point on the inside of the bottom of the "D" handle. It will be at 4" - 4½".

Place all 13 pieces in cool water to soak for a few minutes. Remove them from the water and place three, horizontally, on a table, *wrong side up*, leaving ½" between them.

Next, place the "D" handle on top of the center marks perpendicularly. Then lay four more strips across the "D" handle (horizontally) and between (to the left and right of) the original three pieces. See *Diagram 1*.

NOTE: If all this is too difficult to hold with your hands, lay a heavy book on one end of the reed while you work on the other end.

Weave the other six pieces over and under the seven horizontal pieces, aligning the center marks with the center mark on the handle. Measure and true the base to 8" square. See *Diagram 2*.

Upsetting And Weaving The Sides

To upsett the sides, bend each stake, vertical and horizontal, all the way over (to the inside) upon itself, forming a permanent crease at the base. See *Diagram 3*.

Referring to *Diagram 4*, begin weaving around the basket with a piece of soaked ⅜" flat reed. Make sure the *wrong* side of the weaver is against the stakes. Notice that the weaver wraps behind the stakes that originate from underneath the base. These stakes must stand up first. Weave over and under the stakes all the way around to the starting point. Use clothespins frequently to hold everything in place for the first two rows. Allow the two ends to overlap for at least two stakes. If the reed is extremely thick, shave some of the thickness off where the two ends overlap each other. Begin the next row and every subsequent row on a different side to avoid a build-up.

From the bottom up, our basket is woven with the following materials:

3 rows of ⅜" flat
3 rows of 3/16" flat oval
3 rows of ⅜" flat
3 rows of 3/16" flat oval
3 rows of ⅜" flat
3 rows of 3/16" flat oval
4 rows of ⅜" flat
    (last row covered by rim)

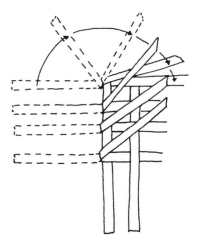

Diagram 3

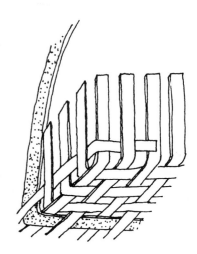

Diagram 4

As you weave, you need to tighten gradually on the weaver and press in on the stakes using the slant of the handle as a guide for how much to bring the sides in all the way around. Make a concentrated effort to round the corners gradually. It's easy to pull in too much around the corners. You want the corners to slant at the same angle as does the handle. Push down on the weavers after each row, "packing" them in as tightly as possible.

If you have any trouble making the sides decrease, place a large rubber band around the tops of the stakes while they are wet. Allow them enough time to dry and your stakes will be pre-formed for you. See *Diagram 5*.

When you have woven about half the height of the basket, you will find that because the sides are decreasing in diameter, the stakes will be pressed too closely together to weave between them. With a knife or scissors, taper the stakes until there is at least ¼" between them at all times. If you wish, you can point the ends of the stakes while you are tapering, since it must be done eventually anyway. See *Diagram 6*.

Finishing Stakes And Applying Rim

When you have woven all 22 rows (or whatever number you choose to weave), you will notice that some stakes are outside the last row of weaving and the alternate ones are on the inside. With scissors or a sharp knife, cut the inside stakes flush with the top row of weaving and taper or point the outside stakes as in *Diagram 7*. Rewet the stakes a little if they have dried out, and bend the pointed ones over and insert them into the weaving (inside the basket). They should hide behind a row of weaving.

After all the stakes are bent over and inserted, place a well-soaked piece of ⅝" flat oval reed around

Diagram 5

Diagram 6

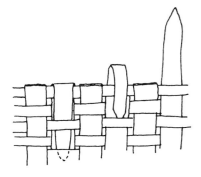

Diagram 7

the outside of the basket, covering the top row of weaving. Allow the ends to overlap approximately 2". This reed is normally very heavy and thick and both ends must be beveled or thinned where they will overlap. The overlapped area should be no thicker than the rest of the rim. See *Diagram 8*. Hold this joint in place with clothespins.

Then, place another piece of ⅝" flat oval around the inside, flat against the top row of weaving. Bevel or thin the ends of this piece just as you did the other. Hold the two rim pieces in place with clothespins.

Lastly, place a piece of #6 round reed above the two rim strips. The ends of the round reed should be beveled in the same manner as the flat oval.

Begin a long, soaked ¼" weaver anywhere, preferably just past the joining point of the two pieces of the rim, and lash the rim pieces all together, following *Diagram 9*. The weaver is inserted under the rim, wraps over the round reed three times, then goes under the rim again. Immediately before and after, and while crossing the handle, you may find that you need more than three wraps around the #6 round reed. When you have wrapped the whole rim, tuck the ends behind a weaver and cut. See *Diagram 9*.

Some reshaping can be done by soaking the whole basket for a few minutes and molding it to the desired shape.

NOTE: *There are other sizes of "sharp top" D handles available. Three are given below with the size reed used, the number of stakes needed and the lengths they should be cut:*

6" x 8" sharp top D: cut 13 pieces 20" long from ½" flat reed

7" x 10" sharp top D: cut 17 pieces 23" long from ⅜" flat reed

10" x 14" sharp top D: cut 17 pieces 36" long from ¾" flat reed

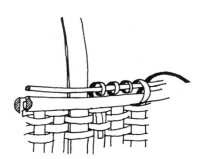

Diagram 8

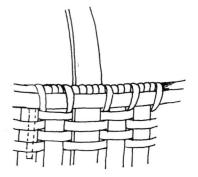

Diagram 9

AMY'S BASKET

TWILL WEAVE MARKET BASKET

TWILL WEAVE MARKET BASKET

The twill or herringbone weave, as it is some-times called, can be used for any flat-bottom basket. However, unlike regular weaving, the stakes need to be flush against each other rather than spread apart.

Finished Size

8" x 12" x 12", approximate

Materials

½" flat reed (stakes and weavers)
8" D handle
½" flat-oval reed (rim)
#6 round reed (rim)
3/16" flat reed (lashing)

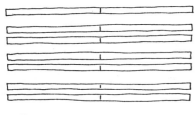

Diagram 1

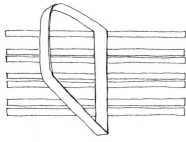

Diagram 2

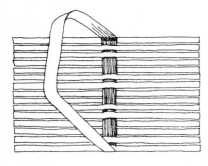

Diagram 3

These instructions will produce an 8" x 12" twill woven basket that uses an 8" x 12" D handle. If you choose not to use the D handle, you can substitute a push-in U handle or swing handles. Instructions for both these alternatives are given at the end. If you want a square basket rather than rectangular, cut all the stakes the same length and use the same number of stakes vertically and horizontally.

Preparing Materials

From the ½" flat reed, measure and cut the following stakes:

> 15 pieces 32" long
>
> 20 pieces 28" long

Mark the center on the wrong side of the reed with pencil. (When bent in half, the wrong side splinters and the right side doesn't.) Place all 35 pieces in water for a minute or two to make them pliable.

Placement Of Stakes

Lay seven of the 32" stakes down horizontally in front of you, with the wrong side up, in three groups of two and one by itself. See **Diagram 1**. Place the D handle perpendicularly across the seven stakes along the center mark. See **Diagram 2**.

Place the remaining eight 32" stakes on top of the D handle (in the same direction as the original seven), in pairs, filling in the spaces between the first seven. See **Diagram 3**. Spread apart or push in all 15 stakes, making the bottom of the basket the exact width of the D handle.

NOTE: This is going to be difficult to hold in place for a while. A large book placed on one end of the stakes will help.

Weaving The Bottom Of Basket

With the fifteen 32" stakes in place, begin weaving across with the 28" stakes. The following guide will tell you exactly how to weave so you will have the twill pattern on the bottom as well as on the sides (O = Over, U = Under).

Left Side Of Handle

Row 1: U2, O2, U2, O2, etc. . . ending O1
Row 2: U1, O2, U2, O2, etc. . . ending O2
Row 3: O2, U2, O2, U2, etc. . . ending U1
Row 4: O1, U2, O2, U2, etc. . . ending U2

Right Side Of Handle

Row 1: O2, U2, O2, etc. . . ending U1
Row 2: U1, O2, U2, O2, etc. . . ending O2
Row 3: U2, O2, U2, O2, etc. . . ending O1
Row 4: O1, U2, O2, U2, etc. . . ending U2

*NOTE: Pattern reads from top. These four rows will be repeated once and you will end with Row 2 (on both sides of the handle), with 10 rows on each side. See **Diagram 4** for the first four rows of weaving.*

Upsetting The Sides

When all 20 of the 28" stakes are woven in, measure and true the base of the basket, making sure it is 8"x12". Mark the corners with a pencil when you are sure of the measurements. (If you are going to have problems keeping the base square, it will be with the corners. If you mark the exact angle, you will at least be aware if any slipping occurs). See **Diagram 5**.

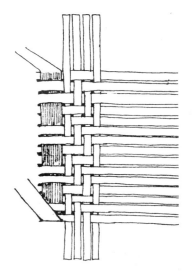

Diagram 4

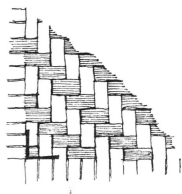

Diagram 5

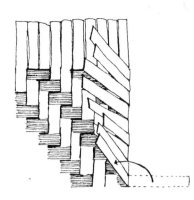

Diagram 6

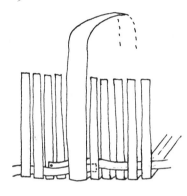

Diagram 7

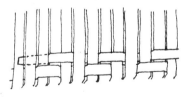

Diagram 8

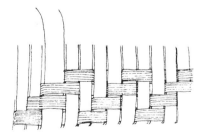

Diagram 9

Upsett the sides of the basket by turning all the stakes all the way over upon themselves to cause a permanent crease at the base of the stake. The stakes will not stand upright until you have woven several rows, but the crease is necessary. See *Diagram 6*.

Starting To Weave The Basket Sides

With a soaked piece of ½" flat reed at least 45" long, begin weaving at the point shown in *Diagram 7* and continue around the basket, weaving over two stakes and under two stakes. Be sure the right side of the weaver is on the outside of the basket. Use clothespins frequently to hold the stakes upright. You will soon realize that you are not picking up all the stakes; only in the third row of weaving will you make all the stakes stand upright.

Move clothespins on the second row of weaving when they are in your way and replace them as needed. When you have woven all the way around the basket and have returned to the starting point, allow the ends of the weavers to overlap to the 4th stake. Check to be sure the ends of the weavers are going to be hidden behind a stake before cutting them. Begin weaving the next row, and every row thereafter, in a different place so as not to create a build-up from constantly starting in the same place.

Refer to *Diagram 8* and begin weaving the second row by inserting the end of the weaver between two of the stakes that were covered by the weaver on the previous row. This is called "stepping up" a stake. You are weaving over one of the same stakes you wove over the previous row plus a new one. Treat the handle as a stake. *Diagram 9* shows four rows of weaving with the twill pattern established.

NOTE: Always remember to begin each row at a new place and to keep the right side of the weaver on the outside of the basket.

Continue weaving until the basket is 6" - 7" deep. Keep pushing the weaver down snugly.

Finishing The Basket

When you have finished weaving all 12 rows (or more if you prefer), you will find that some of the stakes are in front of a weaver and some are behind it. Wet the top part of the stakes again. With scissors or wire cutters, cut off the inside stakes so they are even with the last row of weaving. Then shape the outside stakes to a point, checking each of them to be sure they will reach inside at least to the first row of weaving. Now, bend the pointed stakes over and insert them into the weaving inside the basket as shown in *Diagram 10*.

NOTE: You may need to use an awl to help get the stakes into the weaving.

Applying The Basket Rim

With all the outside stakes pushed down into the weaving (if you are not using a D handle, insert a U handle now), wrap a piece of ½" flat oval reed all the way around the outside top edge of the basket. The flat or wrong side of the reed should be against the basket. Overlap the ends about 2" and cut off the rest. See *Diagram 11*.

If you feel this overlap is too bulky, shave some of the oval side off. Hold the reed in place with clothespins, pinching the corners with your fingers as you go around.

Take a second piece of wet ½" flat oval and wrap it all the way around the inside top edge of the basket, overlapping as before. Hold the two pieces with the same clothespins. Finally, place a piece of #5 or #6 round reed between the two pieces of flat-oval butting the ends.

Lashing The Rim

With a long strip of the 3/16" flat reed, begin to lash all the rim pieces together, as in *Diagram 11*. Use your awl to open the space for lashing, just underneath the rim (below the top row of weaving). Tuck the ends of the 3/16" lashing between the two rim pieces.

If your basket isn't perfectly square when you finish, rewet the whole thing and square the corners by pinching them and allowing them to dry again.

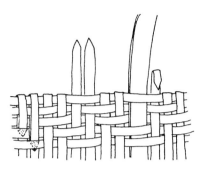

Diagram 10

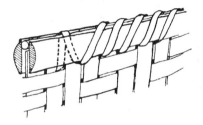

Diagram 11

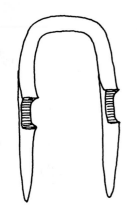

Diagram 12

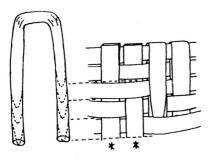

Diagram 13

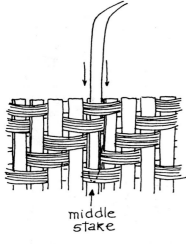

middle
stake

Diagram 14

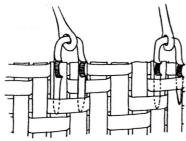

Diagram 15

There are three alternatives for handles that can be used on this basket: D handle (shown in these instructions), swing handle, and "push-in" square notched U handle.

If you choose to use a swing handle, refer to the instructions for Shaker Cat Head or Cherokee Picnic Basket for making the loops. See *Diagram 12*. In this case, because of the twill weave, the loops will need to be long enough to reach the third row of weaving, depending on where you choose to insert them. Consequently, you should decide where they will be placed before cutting them. In *Diagram 13*, for example, one side of the loop will be behind row three, and the other behind row two.

If you are using a push-in handle, simply find the center stake and insert the handle into the weaving before putting the rim on. It can be placed on the inside or the outside of the basket. See *Diagram 14*.

If you are not using a D handle, remember to add an extra vertical (shorter) stake to replace the handle. Begin by laying the horizontal strips and weaving the extra stake in the center replacing the D handle. The arrow in *Diagram 15* points to the center stake. Also, to compensate for the width of the D handle, add two extra rows (one on each end) for length. This means you will cut 23 28" stakes. The 32" stakes remain the same; just be sure the distance across them is approximately 8".

How To Dye Multi-Colored Reed

Coil strips of the reed and tie loosely with a bread tie. For the basket in the photograph we used a peach dye, a blue, and a walnut brown. The coil was dipped into the peach dye at 6:00 until it reached up to 3:00 and 9:00. It was then dipped into the blue dye at 12:00 until it eached to 3:00 and 9:00, and then into the brown dye at 3:00 and 9:00, causing the two colors to be separated by the brown and creating a gradual blending from blue to brown to peach. Any color combinations and any number of colors may be used as long as they overlap each other for the blending process.

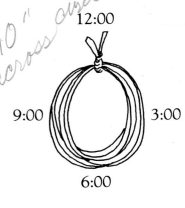

KRISTA'S OVAL BASKET

The photograph shows two versions of this basket; these instructions will make the seagrass version. Try experimenting with your own lengths and widths of reed.

Finished Size

6" x 11" x 14"

Materials

42 ft. ¾" flat reed (stakes)
20 ft. ¼" flat reed (lashing)
54 ft. seagrass (weaving)
10 ft. ½" flat oval reed (rim)
110 ft. ¼" flat oval reed (weavers)
9 ft. #10 round reed (handles)

Shown in the photograph with Krista's Oval is also a variation of it—the swing handle oval, which uses the same technique, flares for about 3-4", then becomes smaller at the top. It is made with ⅜" flat reed for the stakes, six horizontal ones cut 37" long and twelve vertical ones cut 30" long. It is woven with ¼" flat reed, but certainly could have rows of seagrass as does Krista's Oval. The rim is made from ⅜" flat oval reed covering the top row of ¼" weaving. Loops and swing handles are used instead of the wrapped #10 round reed. There are countless ways to vary the basket—be brave and try some of your own ideas.

Measure, Cut, And Weave Bottom Of Basket

Cut five pieces of ¾" flat reed, 33" long. Cut nine pieces of ¾" flat reed, 28" long. Mark the centers of all the pieces with a pencil on the wrong side. Place all pieces in warm water to soak for a few minutes.

Remove from water and place the five longer pieces horizontally on a table with the center marks aligned, about ½" apart. Next, begin to weave the shorter pieces over and under, vertically. Place the first short piece directly over (and under) the center marks on the longer pieces. This is the center stake. Continue weaving the other pieces (four on each side), alternating the over-under pattern. After all the pieces are woven, you should have a mat that resembles *Diagram 1*.

Measure and true the base to approximately 6" x 11", and mark the corner so you will know if any slipping occurs.

Upsetting The Sides And Beginning To Weave

Upsett the sides by bending each stake all the way over (upon itself), creating a permanent crease at the base of the stake. The stakes will not stand upright by themselves, but the crease is necessary. See *Diagram 2*.

NOTE: *The sides of this basket do not stand straight up. You must try to weave around the stakes and still allow them to lean outward a little. Check the shape after each row to be sure you are not pulling too tightly, especially around the corners.*

Soak a long piece of ¼" flat oval reed for a few minutes. Begin weaving around the sides by placing the flat side of the reed against a stake that originates from underneath the woven area. You are now looking at the outside of the basket (in *Diagram 1*, "A" is one of the stakes that originates underneath.) Use clothespins to hold the weaver in place when you begin to weave. See *Diagram 3*.

Weave all around the basket, over one stake, under the next, etc. When you reach the starting point, remove the clothespin and fit the weaver in with the piece already there for three more stakes. Cut the weaver so it will be hidden behind the third stake after the starting point. See *Diagram 4*.

Begin the next row and every subsequent row in a different place so as not to create a build-up from always starting and stopping in the same spot. Referring to *Diagram 5*, make sure the sides are rounded as you weave, not standing straight up. Continue to weave, one row at a time, for six rows.

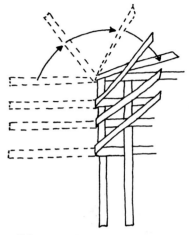

Diagram 2

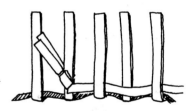

Diagram 3

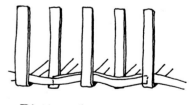

Diagram 4

Diagram 5

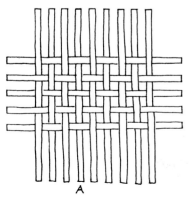

A

Diagram 1

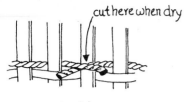

Diagram 6

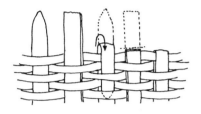

Diagram 7

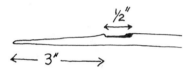

Diagram 8

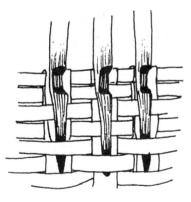

Diagram 9

Diagram 10

On the seventh row, change to seagrass. Soak the seagrass for a few minutes, and begin to weave as before, except the rows of seagrass should begin and end inside the basket. Since they are too thick to overlap, the ends are left free for about an inch inside the basket. When they are dry, clip the ends so they butt. See **Diagram 6**. Weave four rows of seagrass, then six rows of ¼" flat oval reed. Repeat the pattern two more times, ending with eight rows of ¼" flat oval instead of six. The top two rows will be covered by the rim. After the second section of seagrass, begin to tighten on the weaver as you weave to gradually bring the sides of the basket in.

Finishing Stakes And Inserting Handle

When all the rows are woven, finish the stakes by cutting the inside ones flush with the top row of weaving. Then, point the outside stakes, rewet them, and tuck them inside the basket into the weaving. See **Diagram 7**. From the #10 round reed, cut three pieces 27" long. About 3" from each end, make a cut halfway through on the inside of the curve, and then ½" above (toward the center of the reed), make another cut. With a sharp knife, scoop out the reed from this area. Taper the reed from the notch to the end, so the ends are little more than paper thin. See **Diagram 8**. Repeat on all six ends. Insert the round reeds into the weaving, beginning at the third and fourth row from the top. The three handle pieces are inserted with the three middle stakes on each end. See **Diagram 9**.

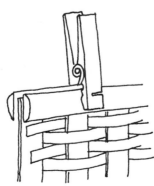

Diagram 11

Applying The Rim And Wrapping The Handle

Wet a piece of the ½" flat oval reed and a very long piece of ¼" flat reed. Place the ½" flat oval on the inside of the basket, covering the top two rows of weaving, allowing it to fit into the notches you made in the round reed. Hold it in place with clothespins. Allow the ends to overlap for about 2". Scarf the ends with your knife so the overlapping area is not too thick. See **Diagram 10**.

Repeat the same procedure by placing another piece of ½" flat oval reed on the outside of the basket. Treat the ends the same way as before. Hold both pieces together with the same clothespins. See **Diagram 11**. Begin wrapping the handle pieces by hiding the end of the ¼" flat reed in the weaving, down between the rim pieces. See **Diagram 12** for the wrapping.

NOTE: If the weaver is not long enough to wrap the handle all the way across, begin a new weaver by sliding the new piece under the old so the end is hidden. Continue wrapping with both pieces until the old one runs out, then continue with the new one. See **Diagram 12A**.

Lashing The Rim

Before beginning to lash the rim, place a piece of seagrass on top and between the two rim pieces. It should lie on the inside of the handle as in **Diagram 14**. Soak a long piece of ¼" flat reed. Referring to **Diagram 13**, from the inside of the basket, bring one end of the lashing up between the inside rim and the basket, over the seagrass, and down the other side between the basket and the outside rim. Next, push the lashing through the first available space (between stakes) from front to back. Continue lashing all the way around with the lashing moving diagonally from one space to the next. Lash in the opposite direction if you wish to create an "X" pattern. The finished rim should look like **Diagram 14**.

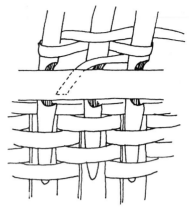

Diagram 12

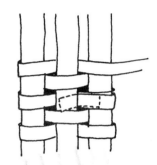

Diagram 12 A

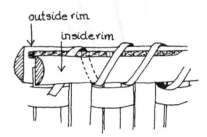

Diagram 13

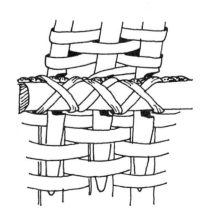

Diagram 14

KRISTA'S OVAL BASKET

POTATO BASKET

This is a nice usable basket that will hold anything you want, not just potatoes. Once you have made the round one presented here, experiment with your own shapes and sizes. Consider using colored or round reed or making an oval one as in the photograph. They are all made by the same basic technique; only the rib lengths will vary.

Finished Size

10" x 10"

Materials

One 10" hoop (rim)
¼" flat reed
#6 round reed

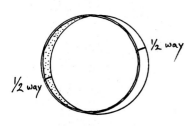

Diagram 1

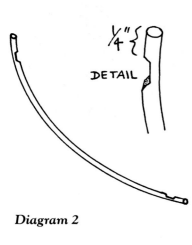

Diagram 2

Measuring And Marking The Hoop

Measure the circumference of the 10" hoop with a tape, then divide the circumference in half, making pencil marks at the halfway points. Hoops vary slightly in size, so each one needs to be measured. See *Diagram 1*.

Cutting The First Three Primary Ribs

From the #6 round reed, cut three ribs, each 20" long. Each rib will probably have a natural curve from being coiled. On the outside of the curve, cut a notch ¼" from the end, and scoop out an area about half the thickness of the rib, and as long as the width of the hoop, being careful not to cut off the ¼" rib end. See *Diagram 2*.

Securing The First Three Primary Ribs

On the two halfway pencil marks you made, fit one of your three ribs on the inside of the hoop — one end of the rib on one mark, the other end on the opposite mark. Tie securely with waxed thread. With the center rib (A) in place, measure and mark 1" to the right and 1" to the left. The other two ribs (C and B) are tied to these marks, just as the first rib is tied. It is crucial to tie these ribs very securely. Trim ends of waxed string. See *Diagram 3*.

Making The Ear

Coil two weavers, separately, each being at least 8 feet long, securing with bread ties or clothespins. See *Diagram 4*.

Soak coiled weavers in water for one to two minutes. Using one of the wet weavers, begin ear. You will be making the ear around the three primary ribs (A, B, C) and hoop (or rim) on both sides of ribs. Begin on the right and make X's on top of the three primary ribs. See *Diagram 5*.

After making X's, and using the same weaver, begin the ear by going around the rim, over C, under A, over B, up and around the other rim. The area between the last rib and the rim must lie flat; a half twist in the weaver is necessary to make it flat, as in *Diagram 6*. Continue weaving ear as shown in *Diagram 7* until you have gone around six times on both rims. Do not cut weaver; secure with clothespins at rim.

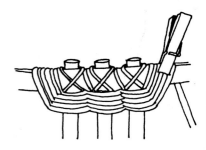

Diagram 5

area to lie flat

Diagram 6

Diagram 7

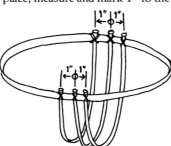

Diagram 3

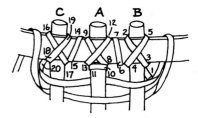

Diagram 4

POTATO BASKET

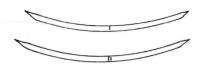

Diagram 8

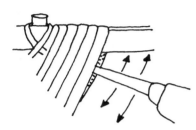

Diagram 9

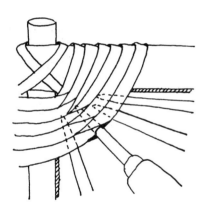

Diagram 10

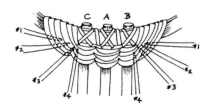

Diagram 11

Cutting And Inserting Other Primary Ribs

Cut two each of the following ribs, and number them as you cut them:

> #1 — 14"
> #2 — 16"
> #3 — 17"
> #4 — 18"

After cutting the eight ribs, sharpen points on both ends with pencil sharpener or sharp knife as in **Diagram 8**.

Insert #1 rib in the first opening, just underneath the hoop, one on each side. Use awl or some pointed tool to open it sufficiently as in **Diagram 9**. Then, insert #2 rib in the same opening as #1, below #1, on both sides. Insert #4 rib in the opening beside C on one side and B on the other side, using tool to enlarge space as above, if necessary. Lastly, insert #3 rib in the center of the lashing by making a space for the rib with an awl or ice pick.

*NOTE: You must actually split the reed between the #2 and the #4 ribs. See **Diagram 10**. This is the area you made to lie flat. If it doesn't lie flat, you will have trouble making a hole in it.*

After you have added all eight of the primary ribs, you have the basic skeleton of the potato basket and it should look like **Diagram 11**.

Measure Opening For Handle

With a tape measure, measure the distance from the edge of one ear to the edge of the other ear. Put a mark at the halfway point. For example, if the distance is 12", make your mark at 6". Then, from the center, measure 2" to the right and mark, and measure 2" to the left and mark. Thus you have measured and marked off a 4" opening which will become your handle. See **Diagram 12**.

Weaving The Basket

After all the ribs are securely in place, begin weaving using the remainder of the weaver with which you made the ear. Simply weave under one rib, over the next, etc., going around the rim and reversing the process making sure your rows are alternating (one row the weaver is over the rib, in the next row the weaver is under the rib, etc.) Weave five rows on the one side of the basket; secure with clothespins. Weave five rows on the other side of the basket and secure. Stop and cut secondary ribs. See **Diagram 13**.

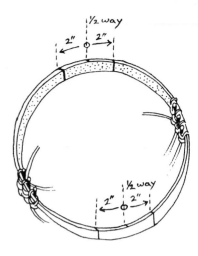

Diagram 12

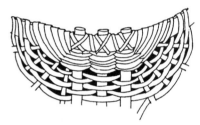

Diagram 13

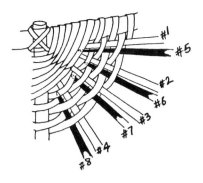

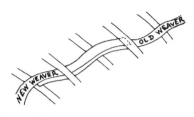

Diagram 14

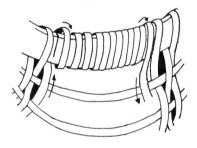

Diagram 15

Cutting And Inserting Secondary Ribs

Cut two each of the following ribs:

> #5 — 14"
> #6 — 16"
> #7 — 16½"
> #8 — 17"

NOTE: The secondary ribs do not go all the way into the ear. They only go into the five rows of weaving, with points hidden under a weaver.

Place #5 secondary rib in the same space as the #1 primary rib. Place #6 secondary rib in the same space as the #2 primary rib. Do the same with #7 and #8 secondary ribs. See **Diagram 14**.

Once secondary ribs are in place and secure, begin weaving again, weaving over one rib, under one rib, just as before.

Do not be alarmed if your over-under pattern is disturbed for the first row. Adding ribs always interrupts the pattern for one row. The second row corrects itself if you always weave over one and then under one.

Splicing

When you have 2" to 3" of weaver left, it is time to join a new (soaked) weaver to it. This joining should not take place at the rim, so back-track if necessary.

Referring to **Diagram 15**, overlap the new weaver on top of the old one. You will be weaving with two pieces of reed for three or four ribs. Hide the ends if possible under a rib.

Finishing The Basket

Continue weaving the basket. Do not weave all of one side, and then the other. Instead, weave several rows on one side then several rows on the other, to keep the basket balanced.

On this particular basket, you must leave an opening in the side for a handle. On the rim you have already marked off a 4" space. When your weaving reaches the mark on each side, the #1 rib becomes the point at which you turn and go back down rather than weaving around the hoop, thus leaving an opening between the first rib and the hoop. Continue in this manner until all the space is filled. The #1 rib will fill in before the bottom of the basket does. When you can no longer fit any more weavers in, drop down to the next rib, turn and go back, just as you turned around your hoop. Continue in this manner until all the space is filled in. See **Diagram 16**.

Wrapping The Handle

This step is entirely optional. If you should wish to cover your handle, insert a short weaver into the weaving behind the rim. Wrap in a continuous motion until the area is covered. Cut the weaver leaving a 1" tail. Insert this end into the weaving on the back of the rim on the opposite side. See **Diagram 17**.

An alternative to weaving the handle opening is given in **Diagram 18**. Simply continue with the weaver wrapping the handle and continue down the other side with the regular weaving.

Try an oval potato basket using the same basic shaping procedure as for the round, making the basket sides round out and the bottom basically flat.

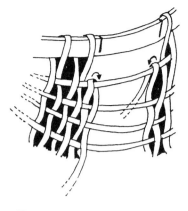

Diagram 16

Diagram 17

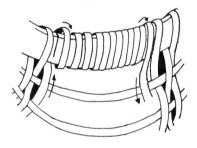

Diagram 18

FLAT-BOTTOM EGG BASKET

It has been my experience from studying old egg baskets that many of them had flat bottoms and ribs were added, two at a time, from the ears outward as the basket was woven.

Finished Size

8" in diameter

Materials

3/16" flat reed (weavers)
1/4" oval reed (ribs)
Two 8" hoops (handle and rim)
 Approximately 30" of #5 or #6
 round reed (lip)

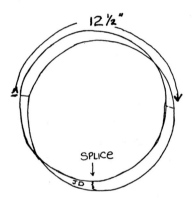

Diagram 1

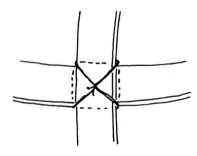

Diagram 2

I found my prototype for this basket at a flea market. I admired it and fondled it, but decided it was too expensive and went home without it. I immediately regretted leaving it behind, of course. I went back the next day to buy it (no matter how exorbitant the price) only to find it had been sold. Because the rim treatment was so unusual, I sought out the new owners who allowed me to photograph it. I'll learn one day to follow my impulses!

Preparing The Hoops

On one hoop, mark off a 12-½" area to be the exposed handle, opposite the splice. Put your initials in the bottom, near the splice, as an identifying mark. Measure the circumference of the other hoop and divide it in half. Put a mark at the halfway mark and push the handle hoop over the rim hoop. The exposed handle mark should align with the halfway mark on the rim hoop. See **Diagram 1**. Tie or nail the two hoops together as in **Diagram 2**.

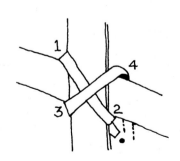

Diagram 3

Making The Ear

Identify the wrong side of a long piece of 3/16" flat reed. Soak and begin lashing as in **Diagram 3**, starting at the dot, and making an "X." Then, as in **Diagram 4**, begin the actual ear by bringing the weaver over the top of the handle hoop, up and around the right rim (6), down to (7), under the handle hoop and up to the left rim (8). Repeat this procedure moving from one side to the other, keeping the wrong side of the weaver against the hoops, until you have five rows on both sides (count from the top of the rim). The finished ear should look like **Diagram 5**.

Preparing The Ribs

From the ¼" oval reed, cut two each of the following lengths and number the ribs as you cut them:

#1 - 13"	# 6 - 12"
#2 - 13½"	# 7 - 11"
#3 - 14"	# 8 - 9½"
#4 - 13½"	# 9 - 8"
#5 - 12½"	#10 - 6"

Taper all the ribs with a knife for at least 1", making them "pencil point" sharp at the ends. See **Diagram 6**.

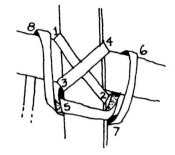

Diagram 4

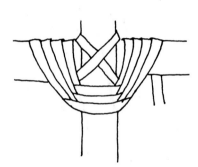

Diagram 5

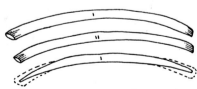

Diagram 6

FLAT-BOTTOM EGG BASKET

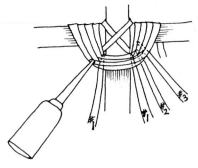

Diagram 7

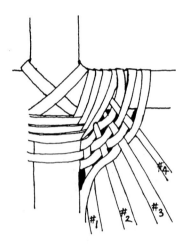

Diagram 8

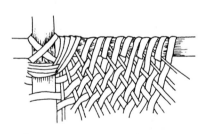

Diagram 9

Inserting The Ribs And Weaving

Insert the #1 ribs into each opening beside the handle hoop, using the awl to open it sufficiently. Next insert rib #3 in the opening under the rim and force it downward. Then, with the awl, make a hole in the center of the lashing and quickly insert the #2 rib. All three ribs inserted should resemble **Diagram 7**.

NOTE: There is no absolute rule for inserting the remaining ribs. You generally add a rib (one on each side) every other row, but whether you insert it after you have finished the fourth row (for instance), or at the beginning of the fourth row, or even after the fifth row is begun is your decision. That decision must be made based on these factors: (1) keeping the "overs" and "unders" in correct order and (2) having the weaver go behind the hoop one round and in front of it the next. Sometimes, depending on how the weaving is running, it is possible for the weaver to go behind the rim twice, in which case you need to reconsider the placement of the rib. Keep in mind, too, that these rib measurements are the ones that have worked for me. They are not sacred and should be altered if necessary. The bottom should be flat. From rib #4 outward, the lengths of the ribs begin to decrease.

See **Diagram 8** for the addition of the #4 rib. When a weaver runs out, splice a new one on as in **Detail A. Diagram 9** shows all ten ribs inserted with the extra turn made around the rim, which is optional.

When all the ribs are in, fold a long soaked weaver around one end of the center unwoven area. Weave with one end of the weaver for a while, then the other. You will be working outward toward the ears. Add the weavers as usual. See **Detail B**. Turn around the other rim and reverse, with both ends of the weaver. At the fullest part of the curve, you will stop weaving "outward" and return to the previously woven area to weave more. Eventually the two areas will meet with very little, if any, filling in to be done.

Making The Lip

To apply the lip, measure from one ear to the other. Cut a piece of round reed that length plus ½" on each end to be pushed between the hoops. Taper the ends of the reed to "paper thinness" and push the ends between the rim and handle hoops as in **Diagram 11**. Also push the end of a soaked piece of lashing between the hoops and begin lashing over the round reed going under the rows of weaving around the rib. See **Diagram 12**.

End the lashing at the other end the same way you began, pushing the other end between the two hoops on the other side. Lash the other side in the opposite direction.

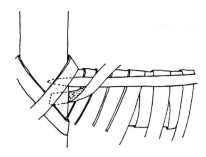

Diagram 11

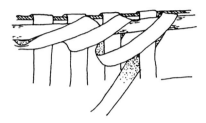

Diagram 12

Diagram 10

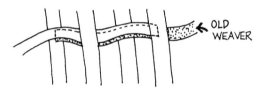

← OLD WEAVER

Detail A

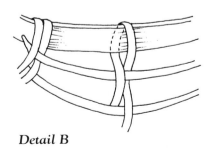

Detail B

SOLID BOTTOM SHAKER BASKET

Inspired by a Shaker market basket with riveted swing handles, this one is smaller and has a stationary handle. The technique for making the solid bottom is unique and very nice compared to other solid bottoms that must be filled in after the basket is finished.

Finished Size

7½" x 11" x 6½"

Materials

⅝" flat ash or reed (stakes)
¼" flat reed (weavers)
⅜" or ½" flat oval reed (rim)
Small square notched handle

NOTE: The layout may look and feel strange because it is done just the opposite of most flat-bottomed baskets, with the longer stakes woven into the shorter ones.

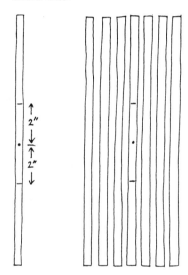

Diagram 1   Diagram 2

The original is shown in the photograph and lengths are given in parentheses if you would like to make the larger one (its measurements are 7½" x 14" x 15"). If you want to use the riveted swing handles, try using a half round rim and drilling a very small hole through the rim for the rivet. Remember the rivet must be long enough to reach through the handle and the two rim pieces.

Preparing The Materials

From the ⅝" flat reed, cut five stakes 21" long and seven stakes 18" long (for the larger basket, cut five stakes 34" long and eleven 29" long). Soak all the stakes.

Making The Base

As in **Diagram 1**, make a center mark on one of the 18" stakes on the wrong side. Then make a mark 2" to the right of it and a second 2" to the left. Lay it vertically on a flat surface. Lay the other six stakes with the marked one, three on each side, all wrong side up. See **Diagram 2**. The distance across the seven stakes should be approximately 7".

Soak a long piece of ¼" flat reed. Begin the base by weaving one of the longer stakes in at the top 2" mark, then beginning the ¼" flat as in **Diagram 3** alternately weaving across the vertical stakes. Leave the ¼" lying out to the side. Do not cut. Be sure to leave a little tail sticking out at the beginning (it can be tucked in later).

Continue to weave ⅝" stakes and ¼" flat rows, alternately. Note on **Diagram 4, Detail A** that the ¼" reed makes a 45-degree turn as it goes around the end of the stake, keeping the wrong side up. **Diagram 4** shows all the rows of ⅝" and ¼" woven. Your base should measure approximately 4" x 7" (the larger version is 4" x 11").

Then, as in **Diagram 5**, weave once around the perimeter of the base. Upon reaching the starting point, pencil a dot on the stake immediately before the first one you wove around, to use it as a reference point.

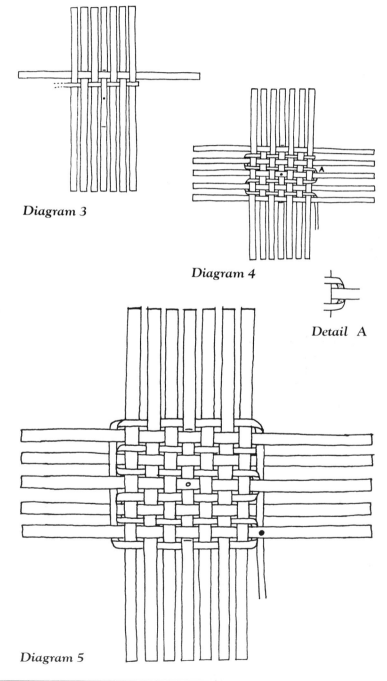

Diagram 3

Diagram 4

Detail A

Diagram 5

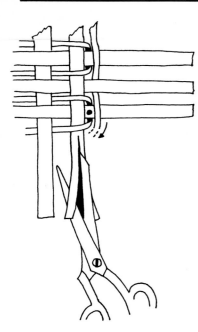

Cut the next stake (after the dot) in half as in **Diagram 6** and continue weaving in pattern, splitting all the corner stakes as you come to them. See **Diagram 7**.

Adding The Corner Stakes

Returning to the dotted stake, cut it in half as well and add an odd stake. To add the odd stake, taper a piece of ⅜" flat for about 4" so it is no wider than ¼" when it is inserted. With this one stake inserted, this corner will have five stakes. The other corners will have six (the two you have already cut in half, creating four, and the two you are going to add as you weave around the next row).

Cut, soak, and mark a halfway point on three pieces of ⅜" flat 12" long. Referring to **Detail B**, taper an area in the center that is about 4" long, making it no wider than ¼" in the very center. As you reach the corners, insert the added stakes by folding the tapered piece in half (with a twist to put the wrong side up) around the weaver. See **Diagram 8**.

Diagram 6

Forming The Sides

Continue weaving for five or six rows and then begin, as you weave, to turn the sides up. Do not upsett straight up; the sides are very gradually rounded upward. By the 8th or 9th row the sides should be upright.

Add new weavers as necessary by the usual splicing method. **Diagram 9** shows an outline of the shape the basket should have.

Finishing The Basket

Cut some of the width from the outside stakes as in **Diagram 10**; rewet them if necessary. Bend all the outside ones and tuck them into the weaving inside the basket. Cut the inside stakes flush with the top of the basket. Insert the handle into the weaving with the center stake as in **Diagram 11**.

Soak enough ⅜" flat oval reed to reach around the inside and outside of the basket and overlap at least an inch. Scarf the ends of the flat oval so they fit together smoothly. Referring to **Diagram 12**, place both pieces of the flat oval on the basket, fitting them in the handle notch, and with a soaked piece of ¼" flat reed, begin lashing them together. Lose the lasher between the two rim pieces at the beginning and the end. Lash only in one direction or in both, making "X's", if you wish.

Diagram 9

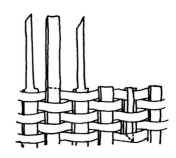

Diagram 10

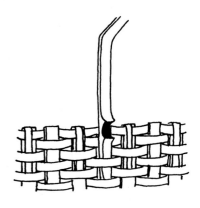

Diagram 11

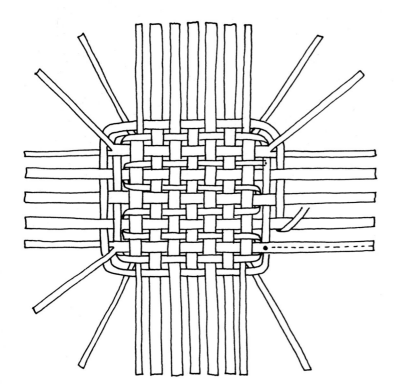

Diagram 7

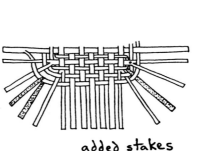

Detail B

added stakes

Diagram 8

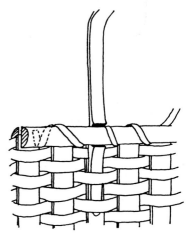

Diagram 12

SOLID BOTTOM SHAKER BASKET

WILLIAMSBURG BASKET

This basket is not made exactly like the baskets that Mr. & Mrs. Cook made for many years in Williamsburg, but it has the same basic shape. Somewhere along the way, someone called this a Williamsburg basket, I suppose just because of the similarity in shape. However it came to be, and whether we are using the correct name or not, it is a strong and handsome basket.

Finished Size

7½" x 12" 10", approximate

Materials

Williamsburg handle
½" flat reed (stakes)
½" flat reed (weavers)
½" flat oval reed (rim)
¼" flat reed (lashing)
#6 round reed (rim filler)

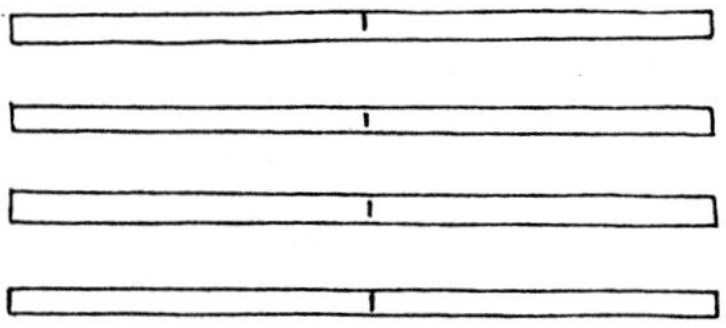

Diagram 1

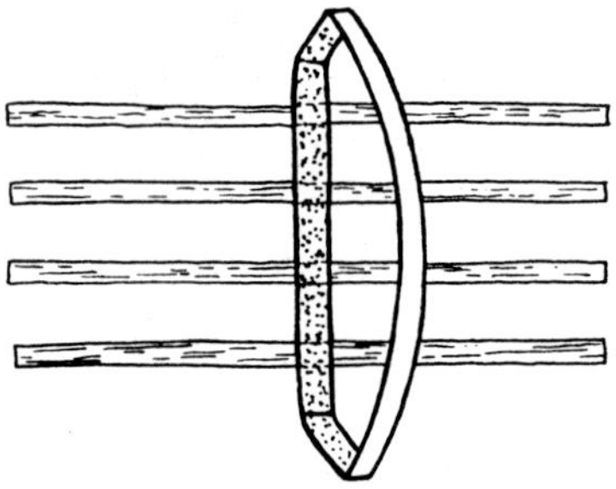

Diagram 2

Weaving The Base And Upsetting The Stakes

Cut 17 pieces of ½" flat reed 28" long. On the wrong (rougher) side, make a mark at the halfway point (half the length). Soak all the strips in warm water for 2-3 minutes. Lay four stakes on a surface in front of you, aligning the center marks, wrong side up. See *Diagram 1*.

Place the handle across the stakes, on the center marks as in *Diagram 2*. Then lay the remaining five stakes on top of the handle in the spaces and on each end. See *Diagram 3*.

With all the nine horizontal stakes in place, begin weaving the other strips in regular over-under basket weave, as in *Diagram 4*. There will be four on each side of the handle. When all are in place, measure the base across all four sides and true the base to 7½" square.

Upsett the stakes by bending them over upon themselves to form a permanent crease at the base of the stake. See *Diagram 5*. They will not remain upright but will stand as you weave around the basket.

Weaving The Basket

Soak a long piece of ½" flat reed. When it is pliable, begin by placing one end of the weaver, wrong side against the stakes, either on the handle as in *Diagram 6*, or on any stake that originates beneath the woven mat (every other stake comes from underneath). Weave all the way around the basket, being careful not to square the corners, and end the row by overlapping the ends as in *Diagram 7*. The two ends are overlapped four stakes, each end hidden behind a stake or a weaver.

Begin the next row and every subsequent row on a different side of the basket so as not to create a build-up on one side from the repetitious starting and stopping.

NOTE: Turning the basket ¼ turn every row is a good idea. When weaving, the sides of the basket supported by the handle will follow the shape of the handle, but you must concentrate on making the other two sides flare out in the same fashion.

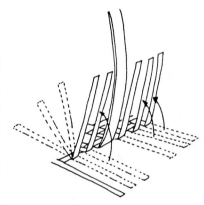

Diagram 5

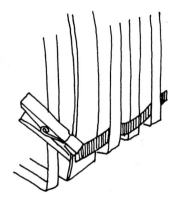

Diagram 6

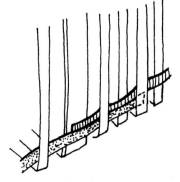

Diagram 7

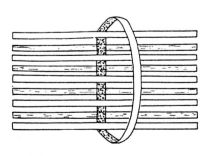

Diagram 3

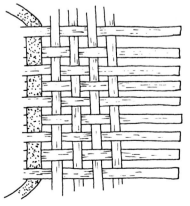

Diagram 4

WILLIAMSBURG BASKET

Diagram 8

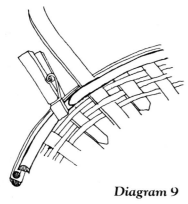

Diagram 9

Finishing The Stakes And Applying The Rim

When you have woven as far as you want (ours is about 10"), find the stakes that are on the outside of the weaving. These are to be pointed with scissors or wire cutters, rewet, and bent to the inside. With the aid of the awl, push them into the weaving as far as they will go. The other stakes (the ones on the inside of the weaving) are cut off flush with the top row of weaving. See *Diagram 8*.

Apply a piece of wet ½" flat oval reed around the outside top of the basket, holding it in place with clothespins. Allow the ends to overlap about 2". Apply a second piece of wet ½" flat oval reed to the inside top of the basket. Hold both pieces to the top row of

weaving with the same clothespins. Finally, place a piece of #6 round reed between the two top pieces of flat oval, still holding all the pieces together with the same pins. See *Diagram 9*.

Then, with a long, soaked piece of 3/16" flat reed, lash all the rim pieces together following the lashing in *Diagram 10*. Lose the ends of the lashing reed into the rim anywhere it is convenient and inconspicuous. You may want to lash in the opposite direction as well, forming "X's" as in *Diagram 11*.

To make the smaller size basket, use the same directions and the following measurements: From ⅜" flat reed, cut 13 pieces 20" long. Weave with either ¼" flat or ⅜" flat reed. Use ½" flat oval reed for the rim.

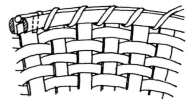

Diagram 10

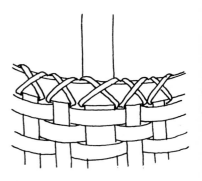

Diagram 11

2. DECORATIVE (BUT USEFUL) WALL & TABLE BASKETS

... Her home was always filled with transient baskets.
Some stayed longer than others, but whether they were permanent or not,
they rarely sat unused.
They served as trays ...
Held the mail ...
or keys on a wall ...
or were filled with fruit ...
or fresh flowers on a table ...

carolynkemp

WICKER FRUIT BASKET

The round fruit basket employs two techniques that are essential to wickerwork — twining and three-rod wale. Once the techniques are mastered, there are many variations of them as you can imagine. This particular basket is shown with one variation and the possibilities for others are endless, as are the uses for it.

Finished Size

12″ x 12″ x 5″, approximate

Materials

#6 round reed
#4 round reed
#3 or #1 seagrass

The directions here produce the seagrass and reed bowl; also shown in the photograph is a tri-colored, three-rod wale fruit basket. The differences between the two are (1) the shape, which you can control, (2) the number of stakes used and (3) the diameter of the base. The tri-colored one is woven around an odd number of spokes while the seagrass version has an even number.

If you are interested in making a tri-color version, start it like the Wicker Plant Basket, using eight long stakes and one short (odd stake), and weave the base about 8″ in diameter. Turn the stakes up more sharply than the seagrass basket and weave all the way up the sides in a three-rod wale, using three different colored reeds. You will see a "spiral" on the outside of this basket whereas there is a "spiral" on the inside of the one made with an even number of stakes. Make the same border of both of them.

Preparing The Materials

From the #6 round reed, cut eight pieces, 40″ long; make a center mark. As in *Diagram 1*, with a very sharp knife, make a split in the center of the reed (on only four pieces) for about an inch. Insert the other four pieces through the splits.

Weaving The Base

Soak a long piece of #4 round reed and begin the base by twining around the four groups. See *Diagram 2* for starting the twining by folding the #4 reed in half and bringing each end over and under the four spokes, alternately. See *Diagram 3* for one revolution of twining.

Diagram 2

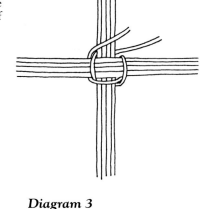

Diagram 3

Diagram 1

After three or four rows of twining around the four groups, continue to twine, but pair all the stakes as in **Diagram 4**. Twine in this manner for 1" - 1½".

Continue twining for three or four rows, but now twine over and under each single spoke. End each weaver by tucking the ends into the weaving beside a stake.

At this point, turn the base of the basket over so you will be working from the outside of the basket; insert the end of a long piece of seagrass behind a spoke ("behind" meaning on the inside of the basket). Soak two long pieces of #4 round reed and insert the ends of each behind the next two consecutive spokes. See **Diagram 5**.

Weaving The Sides

The three-rod wale is done all the way up the basket to the rim. It is done by bringing the weaver farthest to the left to the right, over 2 under 1, and out to the outside of the basket. Continue in the same manner with each "far left" weaver.

All the time you are weaving, press in on the sides of the basket to round and flare them outward at the same time. You must control the shape with pressure from your free hand as well as the tension you use on the weavers.

When you have woven for approximately 6", end each weaver by tucking it into basket beside a spoke. The ends of the spokes should still remain about 12" long.

Forming The Border

The border is accomplished in the following manner: A spoke bends to the right, behind the next one, emerging to the outside. See **Diagram 6**. The spoke to the right follows suit, as does each remaining one.

When they are all on the outside, look at **Diagram 7** for the next step. Each spoke now weaves back into the inside of the basket going under the loop to the right. See **Diagram 8**. Then bring the spokes out again, following the same route as the weaver above. See **Diagram 10**. Then bring the spokes back into the inside of the basket, again following the same route as the one above it. Note that the last weaver goes under all the other weavers. See **Diagram 11**.

Finish the ends inside the basket by cutting them so they will lie smoothly just under the border. Don't forget to go back and cut any ends sticking up where you added a weaver, making them butt each other.

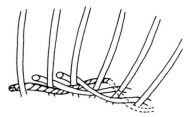

Diagram 5

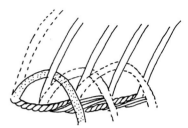

Diagram 6

Diagram 7

Diagram 8

Diagram 9

Diagram 10

Diagram 11

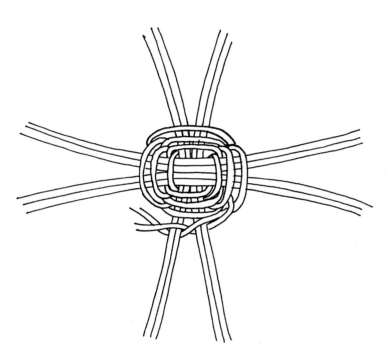

Diagram 4

WICKER FRUIT BASKET

MELON SLICE WALL BASKET

MELON SLICE WALL BASKET

If you have been needing a slim but sturdy basket, perhaps to fit between an inside door and a storm door, this is the one for you. It holds mail, papers, flowers, or other "thin" things beautifully. I'm not sure of its origins, but it's a most unusual basket.

Finished Size

15″ x 10″, approximate

Materials

One 10″ x 15″ oval hoop (handle)
Approximately 4′ ⅝″ flat oval reed (rim)
¼″ flat reed, some dyed in the color of your choice (weavers)
#6 round reed (ribs)

Diagram 1

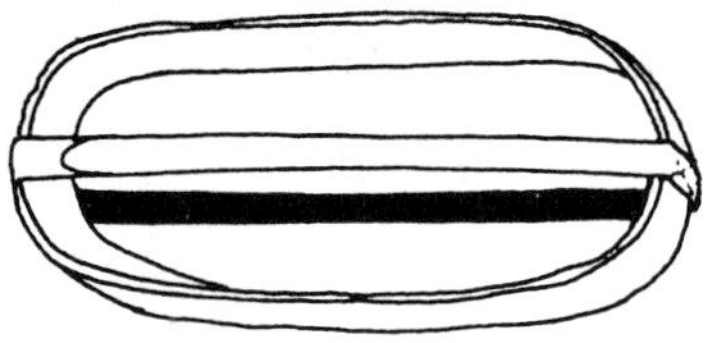

Diagram 2

Applying Rim And Making God's Eye

Cut one piece of ⅝″ flat oval long enough to wrap around the hoop (the long way) and overlap about 4″; it should be about 37″. Shave enough from each end (opposite sides) so it fits together smoothly. See ***Diagram 1***. NOTE: The splice should be on the back of the basket. Soak the piece thoroughly.

Fit the flat oval rim around the hoop as in ***Diagram 2***. Tie it to the hoop on each end and hold the splice together with clothespins.

Soak a long ¼″ flat reed (weaver) for a couple of minutes. Push one end of it between the two spliced pieces as in ***Diagram 3***. Wrap several times around the spliced area to hold the pieces together, wrapping toward the hoop. See ***Diagram 4***.

When you reach the hoop, begin the God's Eye by bringing the weaver up around the handle, down to 3, behind 3, and diagonally to 4. See ***Diagram 5***. From there, make the God's Eye as usual: behind 1, diagonally to 2, behind 2, diagonally to 3, etc., as in ***Diagram 6***. You should wrap for five or six revolutions, counting from the back. ***Diagram 7*** shows the finished ear.

Do not cut weaver. Use a clothespin to secure it at the rim for weaving later. Make a God's Eye on the other end as above.

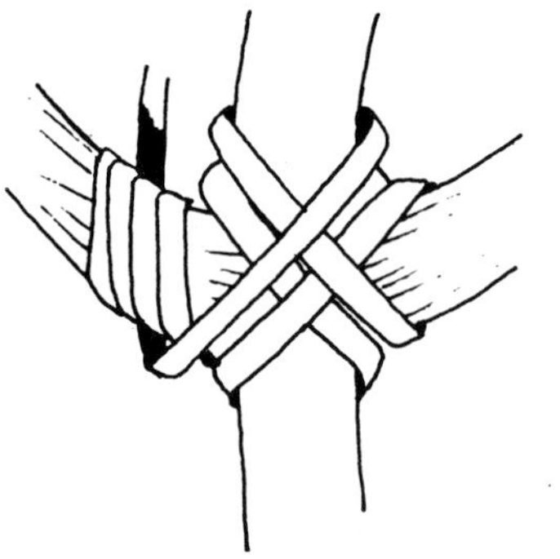

Diagram 6

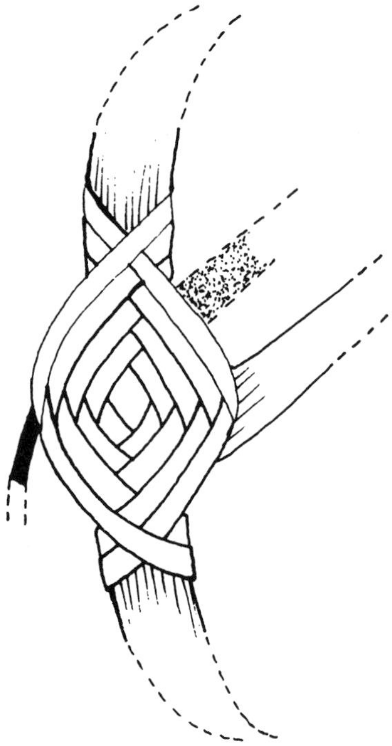

Diagram 7

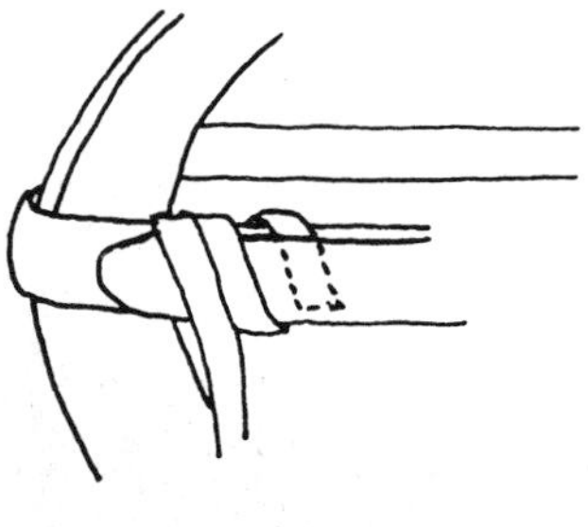

Diagram 3

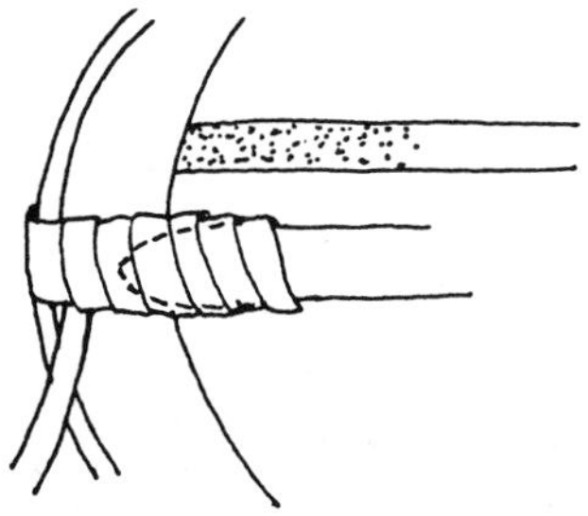

Diagram 4

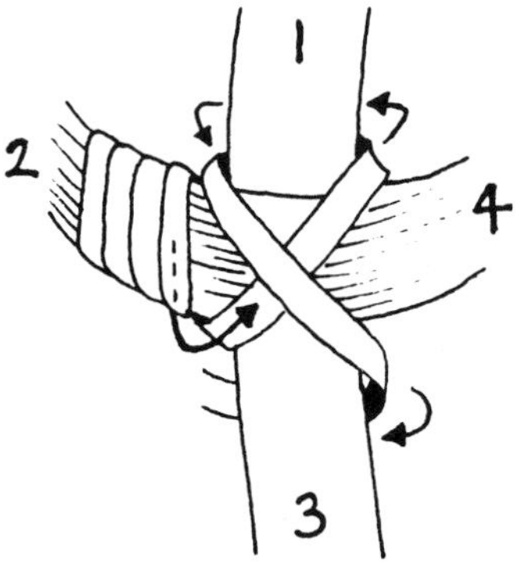

Diagram 5

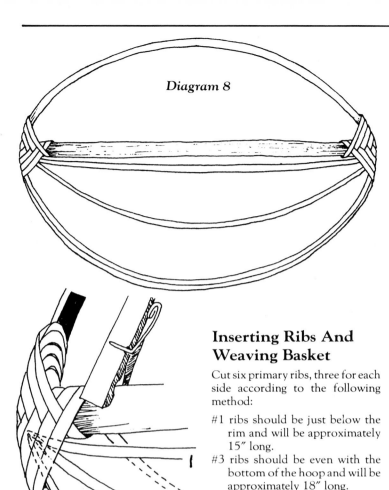

Diagram 8

Diagram 9

Inserting Ribs And Weaving Basket

Cut six primary ribs, three for each side according to the following method:

- #1 ribs should be just below the rim and will be approximately 15″ long.
- #3 ribs should be even with the bottom of the hoop and will be approximately 18″ long.
- #2 ribs should be about equidistant from the other two locations, in the middle of the basket and will be approximately 21″ long. See *Diagram 8*.

Point all the ends with pencil sharpener or knife. Insert them into the "pocket" in the ear, three on each side. NOTE: If #1 rib keeps popping out, make it longer. Another can be added above it later. See *Diagram 9*.

When all the ribs are in place, rewet the weaver and begin weaving as in *Diagram 10*, treating the hoop (bottom) as a rib and turning around the rim on the other side to reverse directions. Weave for four or five rows. Stop and cut secondary ribs. This time the ribs will not be pushed all the way into the ear; instead, push them just under a weaver as in *Diagram 11*.

There are no measurements given for secondary ribs. As a general rule, any time you can get two fingers between ribs, at at their fullest point, you need another rib. The secondary ribs need to fill in the spaces between existing ribs, so where there is 1″ - 1½″ between ribs, insert another rib either above or below the primary rib. On this basket, four secondary ribs added on each side are usually sufficient.

Continue to weave going over and under each rib as before for four more rows. Weave the same number of rows on each end.

When you decide to change to a colored reed, add it near the rim just as if you were splicing on a new weaver. Adding a new weaver is shown in *Diagram 12* and changing to another color is shown in *Diagram 13*. The only difference is that colored reed needs to be started near the rim, on the inside of the basket.

Weave three or four rows of color on each side, as in *Diagram 14*.

Begin a long, soaked, colored reed in the center of one side by folding it in half. As in *Diagram 14*, weave with both ends, turning around the other rim and reversing directions as usual. The two weavers will be moving outward and toward the ears. Weave as many rows as you want in this manner, changing back to the natural color near a rim. After several more rows of natural, resume weaving (natural) from each side toward the center. The woven areas will meet on each side and you will have a small wedge-shaped space to fill in. Do so by either of the two methods given in the Key Basket or Oriole Basket instructions.

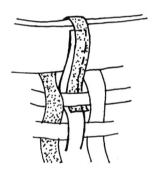

Diagram 13

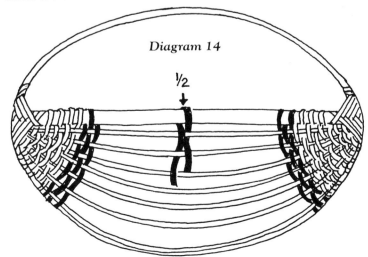

Diagram 14

½

Diagram 10   *Diagram 11*   *Diagram 12*

LIDDED KEY BASKET

LIDDED KEY BASKET

There are a number of different shapes and sizes of the traditional Key Basket. Historically made to hang on a wall to hold keys, there are as many uses for it as your imagination will allow. It can be made vertically oval, horizontally oval, or round.

Finished Size

8″ x 12″, approximate

Materials

8″ Key "D" (frame)
8″ x 12″ oval hoop (frame)
#6 round reed (ribs)
#7 round reed (lid rim)
1/4″ or 3/16″ flat reed
  (weavers)

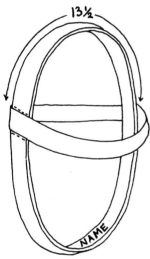

Diagram 1

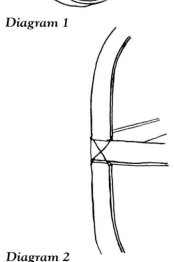

Diagram 2

If you choose to experiment with your own shapes and sizes, simply decide what you will use for a handle hoop and a rim (some type of "D" frame), construct the ears as shown in the following directions, and "sight" the ribs by holding the round reed from one ear to the other, one at a time, until the shape looks "right" to you. Generally, the #1 rib should protrude from the key frame about 1″ in the front. The #2 rib is 2″-3″ longer than #1. The #3 rib is 1½″ - 2″ longer than #2. The #4 rib is 1½″ - 2″ longer than #3. And the #5 rib should lie almost even with the bottom of the handle hoop. The back is easy to "sight" because it is flat and the five primary ribs are about 2″ apart. As with any basket, use your imagination to alter any of the measurements given here, if the shape doesn't appeal to you. After all, you want your basket to be unique and an expression of yourself.

Securing Hoop And Frame

Slide the frame over the 8″ x 12″ oval, not quite halfway. The shorter part of the hoop will be the handle and the longer part the basket. With a flexible tape, measure the handle; it should be about 13½″. See **Diagram 1**.

On the oval hoop, place pencil marks above and below the key frame. At this point, either tie the two pieces together or nail them with a small nail or tack. See **Diagram 2**.

NOTE: A smart thing to do at this point is to place your initial in the inside of the handle hoop on the area that will become the bottom of the basket. This way you won't forget which part is the handle and which is the basket.

Constructing The Bar

From the #7 round reed, cut a piece 19″ long. Make a mark on the reed at the halfway point, another ½″ to the right, and another ½″ to the left. On one end, on the top side, gradually shave away the reed for 4½″ until it is almost paper thin at the very end. On the other end, on the bottom side, shave the thickness for approximately 1½″ in the same manner. Use a knife or a "shaper" for this. Scoop out one half of the reed in the 1″ space you marked in the center of the reed. See **Diagram 3**.

Soak the 19″ piece of #7 round reed thoroughly. When it is very pliable, wrap it around the oval hoop (handle) just above the "D" frame, allowing the shaved 1″ area to fit on the outside of the handle (on one side) and the 4½″ shaved area to wrap around the other side and overlap the other shaved end. Together they should be the same thickness as the rest of the reed. See **Diagram 4**. Hold the bar in place with clothespins.

Weaving The Bar And Making The God's Eye

Soak a long piece of ¼″ flat reed (or 3/16″) until the reed is pliable. Begin by placing an end between the two spliced ends of the bar and wrap three or four times around the two pieces to secure them in place. By four wraps, you should be near the handle. See **Diagram 5**.

Now begin a figure eight movement, wrapping from one side of the bar to the other in an over-under pattern. See **Diagram 6**. When you reach the other handle, begin the God's Eye as in **Diagram 7**, by bringing the weaver around the handle hoop, diago-

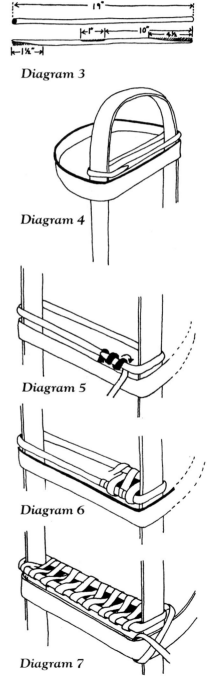

Diagram 3

Diagram 4

Diagram 5

Diagram 6

Diagram 7

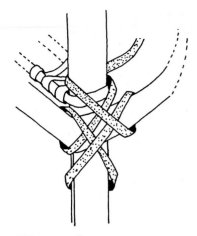

Diagram 8

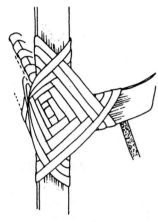

Diagram 9

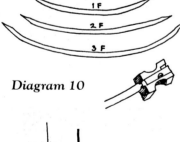

Diagram 10

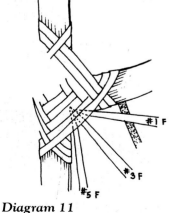

Diagram 11

nally down to the left rim, etc. One complete revolution is shown in **Diagram 8**. Continue wrapping in this manner five more revolutions. **Do not cut the weaver.** See **Diagram 9** for the finished God's Eye.

NOTE: If your weaver runs out before you finish the God's Eye, splice a new one on by tucking a new end under the weaving inside the God's Eye and wrapping over the old end, cutting it at a point so it will lie flat and be inconspicuous.

Cutting And Inserting Primary Ribs

You must cut front and back ribs for this basket. As you cut front ribs, number them with a pencil 1F, 2F, 3F, etc., and 1B, 2B, 3B, etc., for the back. Mark them near the center since you must sharpen the ends and do not want to lose your number in the sharpening.

Cut one each of the following front ribs:
1F - 12½"
2F - 15½"
3F - 17"
4F - 19"
5F - 18¼"

Cut one each of the following back ribs:
1B - 7½"
2B - 9½"
3B - 12"
4B - 15"
5B - 16½"

With a pencil sharpener or sharp knife, sharpen all the ends. The point should begin to taper about ¾" from the end of the reed and eventually become as sharp as a pencil point. See **Diagram 10**.

Insert ribs 1F, 3F, and 5F in the front, pushing the ends into the "pocket" formed by the God's Eye, and ribs 1B, 3B, and 5B in the back using the same "pocket." See **Diagram 11** for the front view and **Diagram 12** for the back view.

Rewet the weavers that were left from making the God's Eye and begin to weave as in **Diagram 13** by going over the first rib, under the second, etc., and treating the hoop as another rib and turning to reverse direction around the rims. Weave three rows on both sides. Stop and insert ribs 2F and 4F in the front. Rib 2F goes under 1F and 4F goes under 3F. Add the 2B and 4B ribs in the back in the same places. See **Diagram 14**.

With the new ribs in place, begin weaving again for two more rows, a total of five rows. **Diagram 15** shows the basic skeleton of the basket.

Cutting And Inserting Secondary Ribs

Cut the following secondary ribs, again from the #6 round reed:

SECONDARY FRONT RIBS:
S1 - 11½" to be inserted below 1F
S2 - 12½" to be inserted above 2F
S3 - 16½" to be inserted below 3F
S4 - 17½" to be inserted below 4F
S5 - 17¼" to be inserted above 5F

SECONDARY BACK RIBS:
S6 - 7"   to be inserted below 1B
S7 - 9"   to be inserted below 2B
S8 - 11"   to be inserted below 3B
S9 - 13½" to be inserted below 4B

Sharpen them all and insert into the weaving according to **Diagram 16**. Remember that every person weaves differently, which can affect the placement of secondary ribs. Alter any of the lengths and/or placements of the ribs you deem necessary.

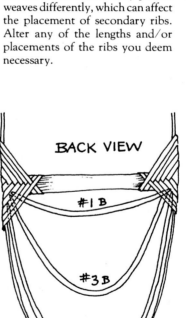

BACK VIEW

#1 B

#3 B

#5 B

Diagram 12

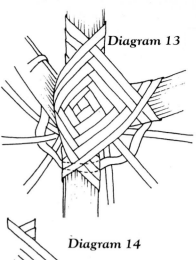

Diagram 13

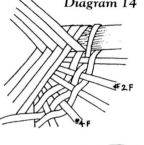

Diagram 14

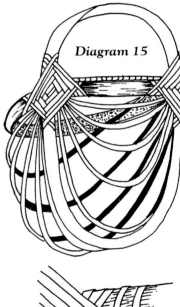

Diagram 15

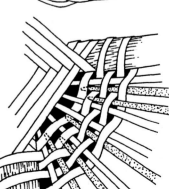

Diagram 16

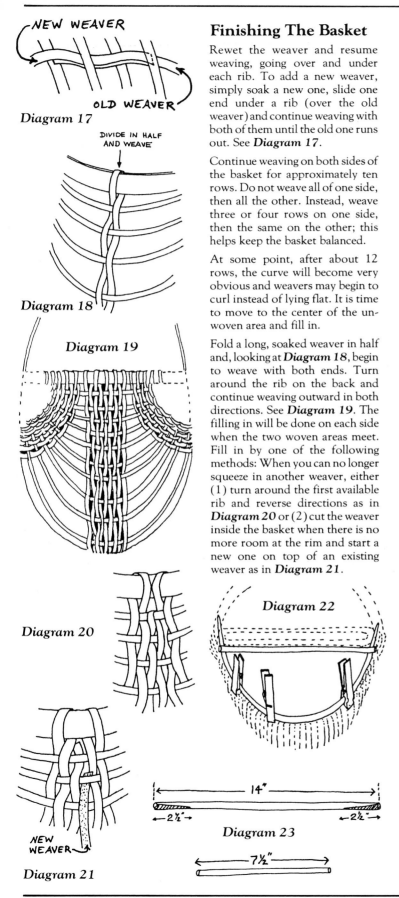

Diagram 17

Diagram 18

Diagram 19

Diagram 20

Diagram 21

NEW WEAVER

OLD WEAVER

DIVIDE IN HALF AND WEAVE

NEW WEAVER

Finishing The Basket

Rewet the weaver and resume weaving, going over and under each rib. To add a new weaver, simply soak a new one, slide one end under a rib (over the old weaver) and continue weaving with both of them until the old one runs out. See **Diagram 17**.

Continue weaving on both sides of the basket for approximately ten rows. Do not weave all of one side, then all the other. Instead, weave three or four rows on one side, then the same on the other; this helps keep the basket balanced.

At some point, after about 12 rows, the curve will become very obvious and weavers may begin to curl instead of lying flat. It is time to move to the center of the un-woven area and fill in.

Fold a long, soaked weaver in half and, looking at **Diagram 18**, begin to weave with both ends. Turn around the rib on the back and continue weaving outward in both directions. See **Diagram 19**. The filling in will be done on each side when the two woven areas meet. Fill in by one of the following methods: When you can no longer squeeze in another weaver, either (1) turn around the first available rib and reverse directions as in **Diagram 20** or (2) cut the weaver inside the basket when there is no more room at the rim and start a new one on top of an existing weaver as in **Diagram 21**.

Diagram 22

Diagram 23

14"

2½"   2½"

7½"

Making And Attaching The Lid

Measure, as accurately as possible, the distance from inside one God's Eye to the other, across the basket at the bar. Cut a piece of #7 round reed the length of your measurement; it should be about 7½".

Next, measure from inside one ear all the way around the rim to the other ear and add enough to wrap around the bar. Be sure the lid will fit on top of the rim and inside the ear; this piece should be about 14". Cut it from the #7 round reed also. See **Diagram 22**.

For 2½" on each end, shave away at least half the thickness of the reed. See **Diagram 23**. Soak the 14" piece until it is pliable. Fold the thinned ends around the straight bar while it is wet and hold it in place with clothespins or cable clips. Soak a long piece of ¼" flat reed and begin weaving the lid ears as in **Diagram 24**. Referring to the detail in **Diagram 24**, insert the weaver between the two pieces of reed and wrap over them two or three times to secure them. Next, begin a two-point lashing around the bar "A" and then around "B" forming a V-shaped ear. You should have five or six wraps on each side. Repeat the procedure on the other side of the lid. Do not cut the weaver. See **Diagram 25**.

From the #6 round reed, cut one each of the following ribs:

#1 - 6½"
#2 - 7¾"
#3 - 8¼"

Referring to **Diagram 26**, insert the three ribs into each ear. If your weaver has dried, rewet it and weave several rows as in **Diagram 26**. **Diagram 27** shows a skeleton of the lid without any weaving done. Weave from both sides, evenly, just as you wove the basket and finish the lid by either of the two methods described in the basket directions. **Diagram 28** shows the lid finished by using the first method given.

The lid can be attached to the bar with a piece of soaked reed pushed through the lid and around the bar and tied underneath. A strong waxed thread, leather, or wire can also be used to join the two.

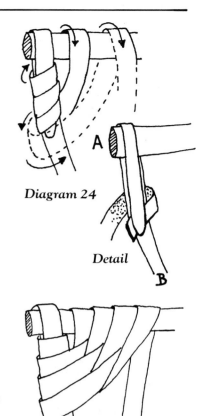

Diagram 24

A

B

Detail

Diagram 25

Diagram 26

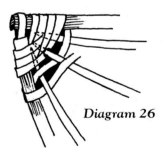

Diagram 27

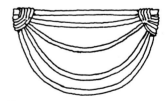

Diagram 28

CHEROKEE COMB BASKET

This is a very useful little wall basket and not necessarily just for holding combs. As with most baskets, it can hold anything that you want it to hold. Of the pair pictured here, one is made of white oak in the traditional Cherokee colors and the other is made of reed.

Finished Size

3" x 7" x 8", approximate

Materials

⅜" flat reed (stakes)
3/16" or 11/64" flat reed, 18" dyed (weavers)
¼" flat oval or half round reed (rim)
#7 or #8 round reed (handle)

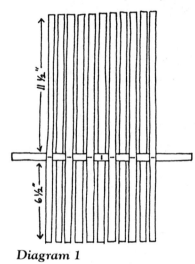

Diagram 1

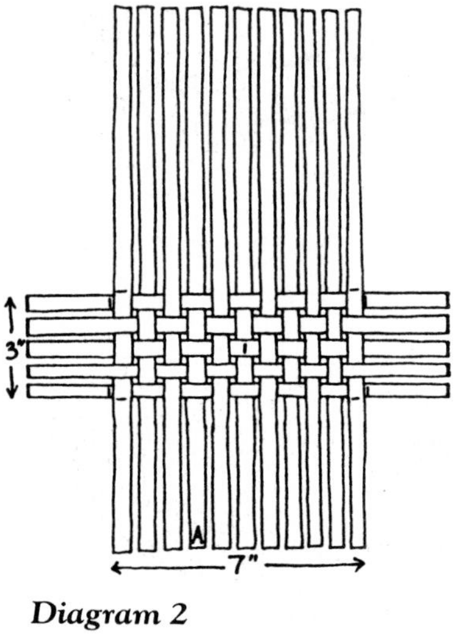

Diagram 2

This style basket is also made frequently by the Maine Indians using brown ash with curls. You can accomplish these as well by using paper-thin ash or very thin reed for the curls. The reed basket is woven with 3/16" flat reed; some of it has been split in half to make extremely narrow weavers.

Cutting Stakes And Weaving The Base

Cut 11 pieces of ⅜" flat reed 18" long and five pieces of ⅜" flat reed 17" long. On the wrong side of the reed, make a halfway mark on the 17" pieces. On the wrong side of the 18" pieces, measure and make a pencil mark 11½" from one end (or 6½" from the other).

Lay the 18" pieces vertically on a surface in front of you, leaving about ¼" between each stake. Align the marks. Next, weave one of the 17" pieces over and under (horizontally) the vertical pieces, aligning the center marks. This will be the center stake. See *Diagram 1*.

Weave in the other four stakes, two on each side of the center stake, alternating overs and unders. Make sure the ends are even and the marks are aligned. See *Diagram 2*.

The base should be 3" x 7". Measure and true the base. mark the corners in case any slipping occurs.

Upsetting The Stakes And Weaving The Sides

Fold all the stakes over upon themselves to form a permanent crease at the base. See *Diagram 3*. Soak a piece of 3/16" reed (natural). Begin weaving as in *Diagram 3* by placing the weaver (wrong side against the stake) on the outside of a stake that originates on the bottom of the woven base (Stake A). Continue weaving over and under all the way around the basket. Overlap the beginning end and continue to the fourth stake. Cut the weaver so it will be hidden behind the fourth stake when it stands. See *Diagram 4*.

Each row will be woven separately. Begin each row in a different spot to prevent a build-up from starting and stopping in the same place. Hold the first row in place with a clothespin or use a "brake."

Weave the following rows in the following colors, or the colors of your choice. See *Diagram 5*.

Rows 1- 3: Natural
Rows 4- 6: Brown
Rows 7-10: Natural
Rows 11-13: Brown
Rows 14-17: Natural

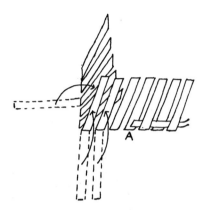

Diagram 3

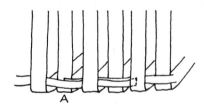

Diagram 4

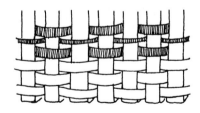

Diagram 5

CHEROKEE COMB BASKET

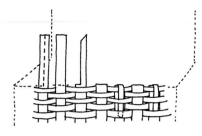

Diagram 6

Diagram 7

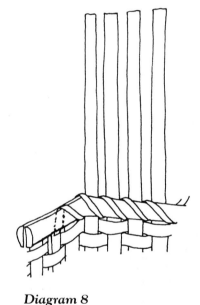

Diagram 8

Cutting And Tucking Stakes On Three Sides And Applying Rim

Leave the long, back stakes standing. Cut the inside stakes on the other three sides flush with the top row of weaving. Point all the outside stakes and tuck them into the weaving inside the basket. See **Diagram 6**.

NOTE: Cut the stakes in half so they aren't so hard to push in.

Place a piece of ¼" flat oval reed around the top row of weaving on the outside. Overlap the ends about 2". Shave some of the oval side off so the overlap won't be too thick. See **Diagram 7**. Repeat the same procedure on the inside. Lash the rim in place with a piece of 3/16" flat reed, as in **Diagram 8**.

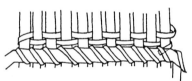

Diagram 9

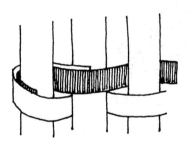

Diagram 10

Weaving The Back

Begin another piece of 3/16" flat reed (natural) by pushing the end between the two rim pieces and weaving across the back. Turn around the other end and reverse directions. See **Diagram 9**.

Change to a brown weaver and refer to **Diagram 10**. Weave five rows in brown, then change back to natural for the final seven rows.

NOTE: Be creative and try changing the number of colored rows, or vary the colors.

Cut the stakes as shown in **Diagram 11** so tucking in will be easier. Bring the weaver around the corner to the back and tuck the stake in over it.

Soak a piece of #7 round reed cut 7" long, until it is pliable and bend it around to form a "U". Mark off a ¼" space on each side and scoop out the reed about halfway through for a notch. Taper the ends so they are paper thin at the very end. See **Diagram 12**.

Push the handle down into the weaving on the back of the basket, fitting the notch around the last row of weaving. Place a soaked piece of ¼" flat oval around the top, fitting it in the notches and overlapping the ends about an inch. It will cover the last row of weaving. See **Diagram 13**.

Start a new lasher by pushing the end into the weaving on the back. Lash the two rim pieces together, going over the handle to the other end. See **Diagram 14**. Lose the lasher at the end of the row, as in **Diagram 15**.

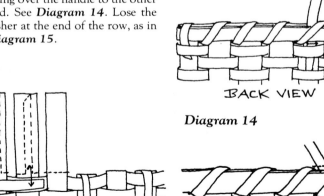

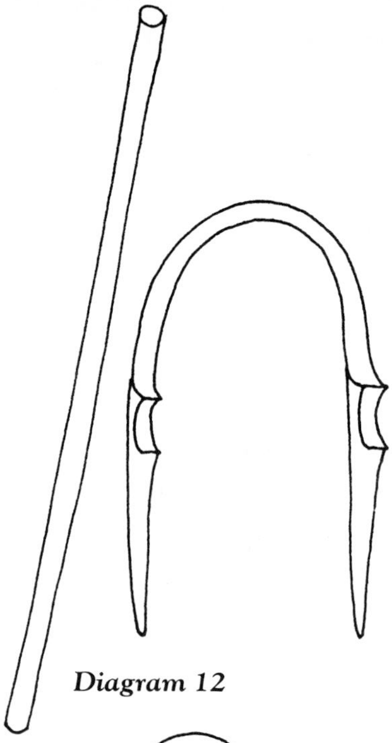

Diagram 12

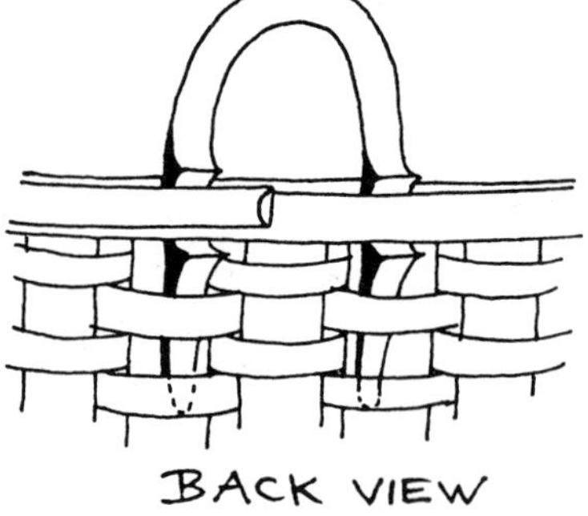

BACK VIEW

Diagram 13

BACK VIEW

Diagram 14

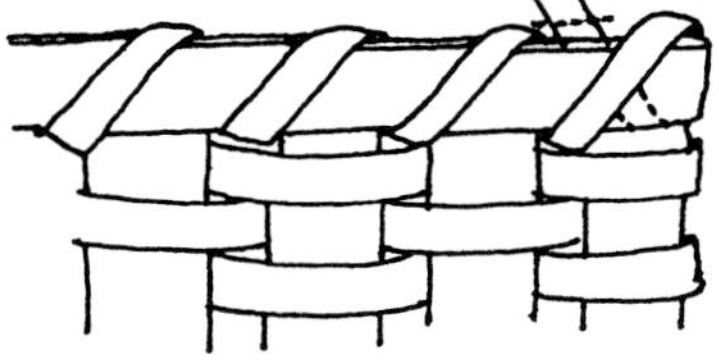

BACK VIEW

Diagram 11

Diagram 15

SHELBY'S MAIL BASKET

This basket is a reproduction of one from the collection of Shelby Underwood. Just because it is called a mail basket here doesn't mean it can't hold any number of other things. Also, it can be lengthened and/or deepened by adding more stakes and cutting them longer.

Finished Size

10″ x 8″ x 14″, approximate

Materials

⅝″ flat reed (stakes)
⅜″ flat reed (weavers)
¼″ flat reed (lashing)
½″ flat oval reed (rim)
#6 round reed (rim filler)
10″ D handle or 14″ high push-in "U" handle

The general directions call for a D handle, but a push-in U or notched U handle can be used instead. *Diagram 8* shows how to insert the U handle, but don't forget that you would need one extra 24″ stake if you use it, to replace the D handle.

Weaving The Base

From the ⅝″ flat reed, cut nine pieces 19″ long and four pieces 24″ long. Mark the centers on the wrong side. Soak all the pieces in cool water for 2-3 minutes. Mark the center of the D handle on the inside bottom.

Lay the four 24″ pieces horizontally on a flat surface, wrong side up. Stand the handle in the place of a 5th stake, aligning the center marks. See *Diagram 1*.

Next weave in one of the 19″ pieces, aligning its center mark with the center mark of the 3rd horizontal stake. Then weave in, alternating weaving on each row, four stakes to the right and four to the left of the center one. See *Diagram 2*.

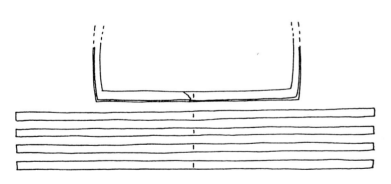

Diagram 1

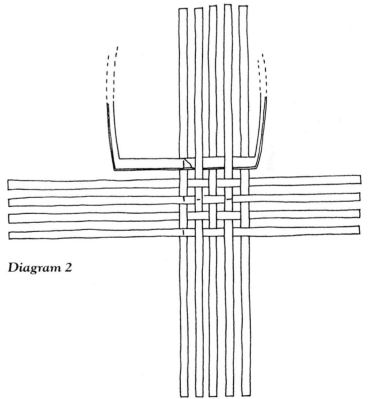

Diagram 2

SHELBY'S MAIL BASKET

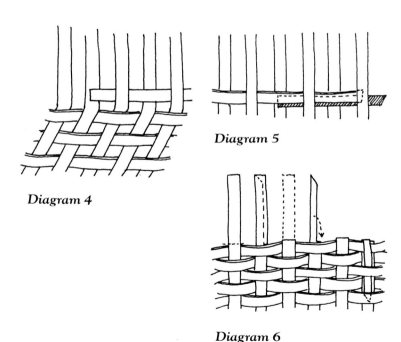

Diagram 3

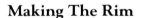

Diagram 4

Diagram 5

Diagram 6

Upsetting And Weaving The Sides

When the base is woven and trued, the sides must be upsett. Bend each stake over upon itself to create a crease at the base of the stake. See **Diagram 3**.

Soak a long piece of ⅜″ flat reed and, with the wrong side against the stakes, begin weaving around the basket by placing the weaver on the outside of a stake that originates from underneath the woven base, and continue to weave alternating overs and unders. See **Diagram 4**. End the rows by overlapping to the 4th stake past the one at which you began (this way, both the beginning and ending "ends" are hidden). See **Diagram 5**.

Begin the next row and each subsequent row in a different spot to avoid a build-up. Weave for 12 rows. Cut away half the width of the outside stakes, point them and tuck them into the weaving inside the basket. Cut all the inside stakes flush with the top row of weaving. See **Diagram 6**.

Making The Rim

Soak a piece of ½″ flat oval reed long enough to reach around the top of the basket two times. Fit the flat oval around the outside top, holding it in place with clothespins and allowing the ends to overlap 1″-2″. Make pencil marks at the point of overlap. Remove the rim, or loosen enough clothespins to scarf the two ends as in **Diagram 7**. Repeat the procedure on the inside of the rim, allowing the two overlaps to be near each other.

Diagram 8 shows where to insert a push-in handle if you haven't used a D handle.

Place the #6 round reed between the two rim pieces, as in **Diagram 9**.

Begin a soaked lasher by losing the end between the rim pieces, as in **Diagram 10**, and lash all the way around the basket in one direction. If you wish, lash in the opposite direction to make an "X" lashing, losing the lasher at the end as well.

Diagram 7

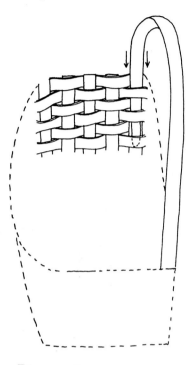

Diagram 8

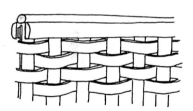

Diagram 9

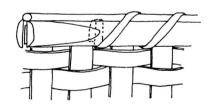

Diagram 10

WEED BASKET

Everyone who has seen this little basket likes it. It will hold weeds, candles, toothbrushes — absolutely anything that will fit. Credit for the design must go to Judy Wobbleton, who makes and sells hundreds of them and is as neat as the basket!

Finished Size

5″ x 6½″

Materials

½″ flat reed (stakes)
¼″ flat reed, natural (weavers)
¼″ flat reed, colored (weavers)
  (optional)
#2 round reed (twining)
10″ seagrass (rim filler)
Wood heart and twine (optional)

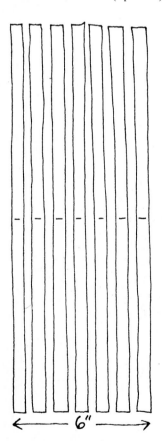

← 6″ →

Diagram 1

Weaving The Basket

Cut seven pieces of ½″ flat reed 18″ long. Soak them all for a couple of minutes. Mark the centers on the wrong side. Lay the seven soaked pieces vertically on a surface in front of you, leaving ¼″-⅜″ between the stakes. Lay them wrong side up. See *Diagram 1*.

Soak a long piece of #2 round reed. Begin twining on the left side a little below the center line. In twining, one end of the reed goes over a stake while the other end goes under. The two pieces are opposite on the next stake. See *Diagram 2*.

Twine back and forth turning at the end and reversing direction. Twine for four rows ending at the 5th stake, which should be cut in half (lengthwise) down to the twining. (The side with the split stake will be the back of the basket.) See *Diagram 3*.

Fold the two sides of the basket up, letting the twining become the bottom. For about 3″ taper one end of a soaked ¼″ flat reed (natural) to approximately ⅛″ in width and begin weaving around the basket by inserting the narrow end into the split stake (see *Diagram 4*) and continuing around the basket, bringing the two sides together enough so that there isn't a hole on the ends. *Diagram 5* shows two rows of weaving in place with the sides upright and the twining in the bottom.

Weave continuously for 16 rows; continuous weaving is possible because of the odd number of stakes. You must control the shape of the basket; do not allow it to pull in too quickly. Pressing on the ends (seams) will cause your basket to become round. The top opening should be round and about 4″ in diameter.

INSIDE VIEW OF BACK

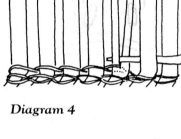

Diagram 4

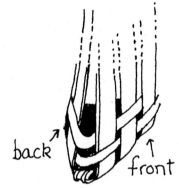

back   front

Diagram 5

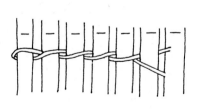

Diagram 2

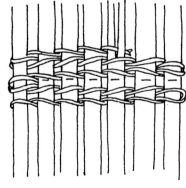

Diagram 3

WEED BASKET

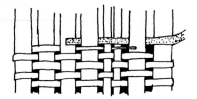

Diagram 6

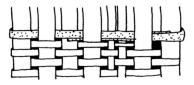

Diagram 7

After 16 rows, again taper the end of the weaver and let it end at the split stake. See **Diagram 6**.

Soak the colored reed for a couple of minutes. Wipe the whole length of it with a cloth or paper towel to be sure that no dye will run onto the natural reed. Begin weaving with the new piece, going over the two parts of the split stake, **treating them as one again**. See **Diagram 7**. **Diagram 8** shows what the basket should look like at this point. Weave three rows, each row individually, with the colored reed, then change back to the natural reed for four rows, continuing to weave one row at a time. Continue, also, to treat the split stake as one.

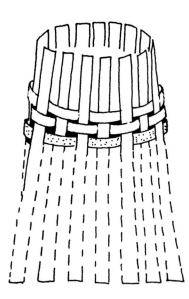

Diagram 8

Finishing The Stakes And Applying The Rim

Finish the stakes by cutting the ones on the inside flush with the top row of weaving. Point all the outside stakes and tuck them into the weaving on the inside of the basket, as in **Diagram 9**. Insert a piece of ¼″ flat reed, natural or colored, as in **Diagram 10**, looping the ends under the second weaver and twisting it at the top.

Next, place a piece of soaked ½″ flat reed around the outside top, covering the top two rows of ¼″ weaving and overlapping the ends 1″-2″. Hold this reed in place with clothespins. Do the same thing on the inside, creating a two-piece rim. On top and between the two rim pieces, lay a piece of seagrass. Overlap the ends a little for the moment. See **Diagram 11**.

Begin lashing just past the spliced area of the rim by pushing one end of the soaked lasher down between the rim pieces (called "losing the lasher") and lash over all the rim pieces, going into each space between the stakes. When you have lashed to within 1″ of the splice, cut the seagrass so that the ends butt together and then finish by losing the lasher again.

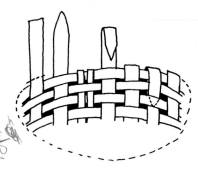

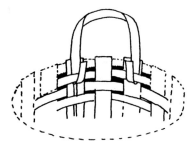

Diagram 9

Diagram 10

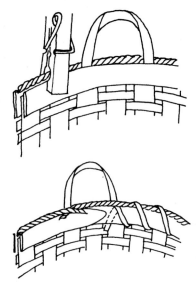

Diagram 11

HERB BASKET

Although this basket is historically called an Herb Basket, it is often called a "pie carrier" these days, because, logically, it is the right size for a pie plate. Whatever its name or use, it is a lovely basket and relatively easy to construct.

Finished Size

10″ x 10″, approximate

Materials

Herb frame (short "D" handle)
10″ hoop (frame)
#6 round reed (rib)
3/16″ or 1/4″ flat reed (weavers)
1-2 yards of ⅜″ flat reed
   (bow-knot ear)

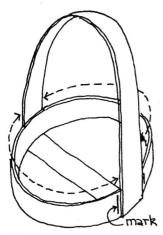

Diagram 1

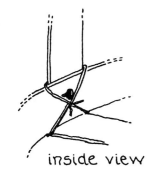

Detail A

The handle is very similar to a "D" handle. It is usually found in 6″, 8″, 10″, and 12″ diameters and is several inches shorter than a "D" handle. The hoop is the same diameter as the handle. The basket is very shallow, of course, but a 1″-2″ wide handle works best. It is somewhat different from other ribbed baskets in that you only weave a bottom.

Securing Hoop And Handle

Place the hoop inside the handle. Tie the hoop in place with twine or waxed thread. Measure (with a flexible tape measure) from one side of the hoop to the other (on both sides) to make sure the distance is the same. Make adjustments, if necessary, by sliding the hoop. Make a pencil mark on each side of the handle so you will know if the hoop moves. See **Diagram 1**. Nail the two pieces together with a small nail or tack. The string can be removed after nailing. See **Detail A**.

Place two strips of ⅜″ flat reed (each about 18″ long) in warm water to soak while reading through the next step.

Constructing The Bow-Knot Ear

Using a piece of soaked ⅜″ flat reed, place the wrong side against the handle and begin at the dot. The "wrong" side of the reed is the rougher, hairy side. Construct the ear, referring to **Diagrams 2-6** and the following pattern:

From the dot, move up to 1 and down inside to 2, up to 3, covering end of weaver, behind handle to 4. See **Diagram 2**. Go down to 5 (**Diagram 3**), up to 6, twisting the weaver (on the inside) to put the wrong side on top. See **Diagram 4**. Go down through the "X" you made to 7 (**Diagram 3**), up in front and down through the "X" again (**Diagram 5**). Pull the end of the weaver tightly and cut it at the bottom of the rim. The finished ear should look like **Diagram 6**.

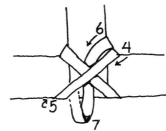

Diagram 3

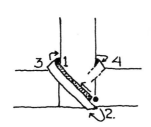

Diagram 2

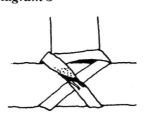

Back view

Diagram 4

Inserting Primary Ribs

There are six primary ribs in this bottom, three on each side of the handle base. You must make holes in the ⅜″ reed for all these ribs. See **Diagram 7** for placement of the ribs.

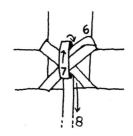

Diagram 5

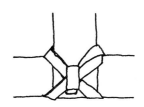

Diagram 6

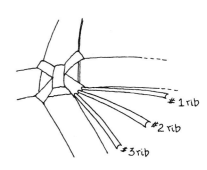

Diagram 7

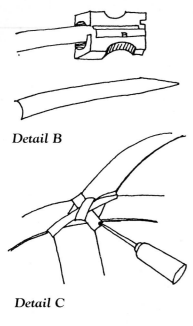

Detail B

Detail C

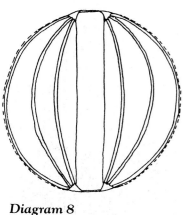

Diagram 8

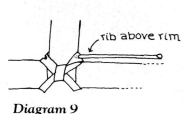

rib above rim

Diagram 9

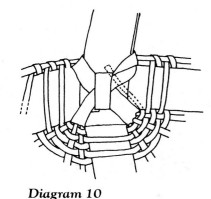

Diagram 10

Using a pencil sharpener or sharp knife, point one end of a piece of #6 round reed (use #5 for smaller baskets). See **Detail B**. With the awl make a hole in the ⅜″ reed near the rim. See **Detail C**. Insert the sharp point into the hole you made and hold the rib around the edge of the rim, sliding your fingers around the two pieces together all the way to the other ear, to be sure the rib is exactly parallel with the rim.

Allow ¼″ for sharpening. Mark, cut, sharpen, and insert into the ear. Repeat the procedure for the other side of the basket.

The second rib is easy to "sight." It is about 3″ shorter than the first. Make a hole in one ear, sharpen one end of round reed again, and insert and hold the reed around to the other side, "sighting" it to be about 3″ from the first one. Repeat procedure used on the first two ribs.

Then cut a third rib about 2″ shorter than the second. Insert on both sides. See **Diagram 8** for spacing of all six primary ribs.

Also, most people like to put a rib above the rim of the basket, for no other reason than to give the basket more depth; two may be added if you prefer. Use the same procedure to measure this rib as for the others. This rib is inserted also into the ⅜″ flat reed, with the aid of the awl, above the rim. See **Diagram 9**.

Beginning To Weave

A very narrow 3/16″ weaver is necessary for weaving this basket. If you don't have a scant 3/16″, then use scissors and split a long strip of ¼″ flat in half to use for at least the first five rows. As you move toward the fullest part of the basket, you can change to a larger weaver. The old herb baskets were woven entirely with weavers usually no wider than ⅛″. The weaving will be nicer and tighter if you have the patience to weave the entire basket with ⅛″.

Begin by tucking the end of the weaver behind the ear anywhere it will stay securely. Bring it over the first rib, under the second, over the third, under the handle base, over the third rib on the other side, etc. Continue all the way to the rib

above the rim. Go around the top rib and reverse directions. Continue weaving in the opposite direction, this row weaving over the "unders" and under the "overs." Continue for five or six rows. Be sure to count each row separately (not from the rim). See **Diagram 10**.

Splicing A New Weaver

When you have 2″ or 3″ of the weaver remaining, you need to splice on a new one. Referring to **Diagram 11**, simply lay a new, wet weaver on top of the old one, hiding the ends under a rib. Weave with both until the old one runs out. Continue with the new one. You never want to add a new weaver on the rim. If you foresee this happening, backtrack a few ribs to avoid it.

Adding Secondary Ribs

On a 10″ herb basket, you will need to add six more ribs, three on each side. You can also easily "sight" these ribs, holding a piece of round reed from one side, curving to the other side, and making sure the ends will reach only into the weaver, not into the ear. The ends of the secondary ribs need only to be hidden under the first available weaver. See **Diagram 12** for placement of the secondary ribs. Each secondary rib will be placed underneath the corresponding primary rib, in the same space with the primary rib.

NOTE: An 8″ basket will need only four secondary ribs and a 6″ basket may need only the three primary ribs. Use our "rule of thumb" for adding secondary ribs: If you have more than 1″ between any two ribs, at their fullest point, you need to add.

Finishing The Basket

Continue weaving from one side of the basket to the other, on both ends, until the handle base fills in. Push the weaving outward, toward the ears, and squeeze weavers in across the base until you can no longer get another one in. When it is absolutely full, turn around the nearest rib, reversing the direction of the weaving. You are now working with only one side at a time.

Continue to weave to the rim and back to the first available rib, reversing around that rib, until the V-shaped area fills in. See **Diagram 13**.

To begin weaving the second unfilled side, simply hide the end of a weaver under a rib or the handle base and begin a new row. See **Detail D**. Remember to rewet the weaver anytime it feels dry. When the entire bottom is filled in, clip any hairs or splinters, and stain your completed basket if you desire.

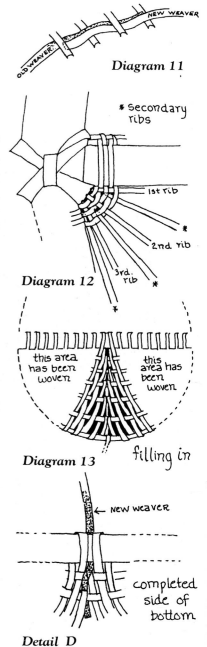

Diagram 11

✱ secondary ribs

1st rib

2nd rib

3rd rib

Diagram 12

this area has been woven

this area has been woven

Diagram 13

filling in

NEW WEAVER

completed side of bottom

Detail D

HERB BASKET

TWINED PLANTER

Woven around an odd number of spokes, a slightly larger version of these directions makes a wonderful wastebasket. Consider varying the sizes and lengths of the round reed to produce a basket to hold a particular flower you might have.

Finished Size

10″ in diameter

Materials

#5 round reed
#4 round reed
#3 round reed (some natural and some dyed three shades of any color)

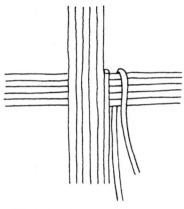

Diagram 1

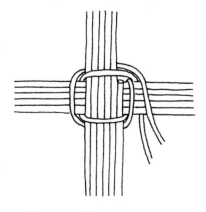

Diagram 2

Preparing The Materials

From the #5 round reed, cut 20 pieces that are 39″ long. Cut one piece that is 19″ long. Soak all of them along with two or three long pieces of #3 round reed.

Lay five pieces horizontally (centers marked) with the other five on top, vertically. Add the short spoke on top with the other five as in *Diagram 1*.

Making The Base

Begin twining around the four sections of reed by folding a soaked piece of #3 round reed in half and sliding it around one of the horizontal groups. See *Diagram 2*.

Remember that in twining, the piece that was on top the last row, is under the next, always picking the top piece up first and moving it under the next spoke.

When one reed runs out, simply lay a new soaked piece beside the old one allowing the two ends to overlap an inch or more. Go back later and cut them so they butt. See *Diagram 3*.

Twine around the four groups four times. On the 5th row, cut one of the weavers, tuck it under the woven area discreetly, and continue with the one weaver in a simple over one-under one wicker weave, now pairing all the spokes except the odd one. Weave it as a "single." See *Diagram 4*.

Weave for seven rows or about 1″, then split all the pairs, now weaving over and under each spoke. Continue for another ½″ approximately, and change to a soaked #4 weaver. Continue the wicker weave for the rest of the base which should be about 7″ in diameter. See *Diagram 5*.

When the base is finished, end the weaver by tucking it into the weaving beside a spoke. See *Diagram 6*.

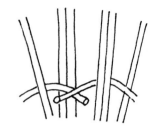

Diagram 3

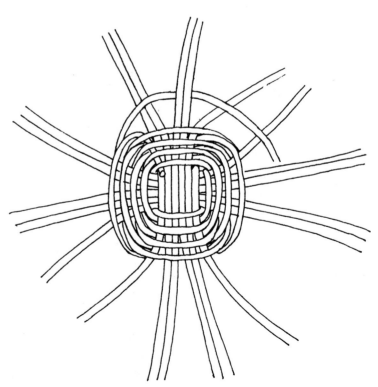

Diagram 4

Weaving The Basket

All the while you have been weaving, the edges of the base have had a tendency to curve upward. At this point turn the base over so the center is convex (giving the basket a "ring" to sit on). Resoak the spokes. Bend them upward, in the same direction as the curve of the base, to create the sides of the basket. Make sure the center of the base (inside the basket) is raised. See **Diagram 7**.

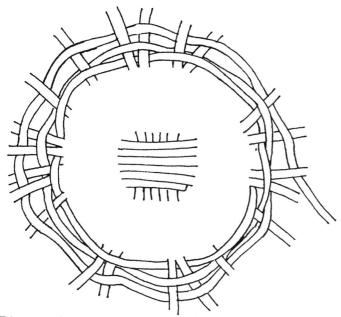

Diagram 5

Diagram 6

Start two new pieces of #4 round reed at the base ending point and working from the outside of the basket, begin twining around each spoke. See **Diagram 8**. Twine for about 2″. Keep an eye on the shape your basket is assuming; the sides should rise straight up. After 2″, end the two pieces of #4 reed by tucking them down into the weaving beside a spoke, above the starting point.

Soak the colored #3 reed. Begin (above the previous endings) three pieces of your colored reed, one of each shade, behind three consecutive spokes, and begin a three rod wale. See **Diagram 9**.

The reed to the far left moves to the right, over two spokes, behind the 3rd and to the outside. Continue with your second new piece now the farthest to the left. Work the three rod wale for 1½″ to 2″. End the three pieces just as you began, letting them "lie" inside, behind three consecutive spokes, above the starting point.

Making The Border

Return to the #4 reed and resume twining for about 2″ more. Resoak the ends of the spokes well. Pack all the weaving down as tightly as you can.

Make the border according to **Diagram 10** by bringing a spoke over to the right, behind two spokes, in front of the next two, and resting behind the 5th spoke. Follow the same procedure with the spoke to the right and with each one thereafter. The last spoke will be a little difficult, but try to ignore everything that is woven and follow the same pattern.

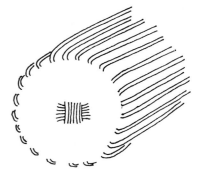

Diagram 7

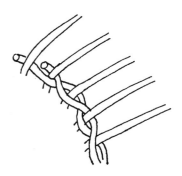

Diagram 8

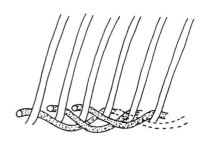

Diagram 9

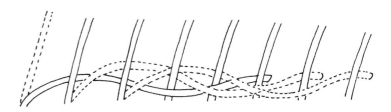

Diagram 10

TWINED PLANTER

CHOCTAW POUCH

CHOCTAW POUCH

This basket, or versions of it, appears in the work of several Indian tribes, but apparently is most often attributed to the Choctaw Indians. Frankly, it gave me a fit in the beginning, but once the diagonal technique registers, it's a snap. This is probably one of the simpler pattern designs and I am told that you can create your own patterns with some experimentation.

Finished Size

12″ x 9″ x 16″, approximate

Materials

½″ flat reed (stakes and weavers)
½″ flat oval (rim)
¼″ flat reed (lashing and handle wrap)
#5 round reed (rim filler)
30″ of ⅜″ flat reed (handle)

Cutting Weavers And Weaving The Base

From the ½″ flat reed, cut 23 pieces 28″ long. In the color of your choice, dye 11 strips. Rinse thoroughly and wipe off any excess dye that might bleed. Soak the remaining 12 strips. Mark a half-way point on the natural strips on the wrong side. See *Diagram 1*.

Diagram 1

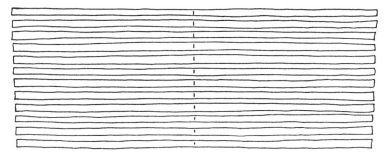

On the wrong side of the colored strips, make a pencil mark at 7½″ (from one end) and another mark 14″ from the other end (this is the center). Begin twill weaving the 11 colored pieces at the center mark on the natural stakes, and following *Diagram 2* move to the left. Be sure the first stake weaves under 2, over 2, etc. NOTE: The base is shown very loosely woven for clarity only. In reality the stakes should be flush against each other.

Weaving The Basket

As in *Diagram 3*, roll the natural stakes over the woven area (**do not crease**) the natural stakes over the woven area. They won't be easy to hold in place, but use a weight on the very ends if you need to; just don't fold them flatly.

Then, as in *Diagram 4*, begin twill weaving the colored stakes into the natural ones. Be very sure to follow the diagram. Make a mental note of the asterisk at the lower right

corner; this will become the point at the bottom of the basket.

Continue weaving all the colored stakes into the natural ones, stepping up one stake each row. When you finish weaving all the colored stakes into the natural ones, your square should look like *Diagram 5*.

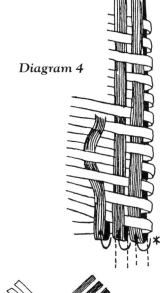

Diagram 4

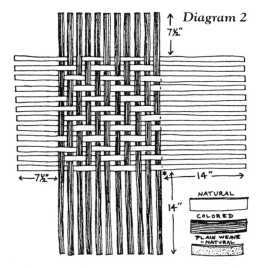

Diagram 2

7½″

7½″   14″

NATURAL
COLORED
PLAIN WEAVE - NATURAL

14″

14″

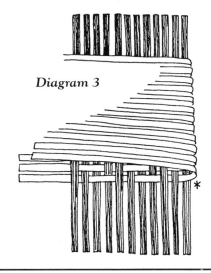

Diagram 3

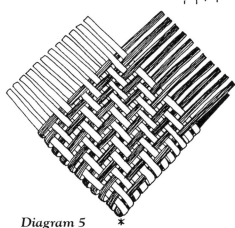

Diagram 5

Forming The Basket

Assuming that you are looking down into the basket, *Diagram 6* illustrates the movement that you must make with this basket. The drawing on the left is the shape you have now. Hold the basket on the sides at points A and C and, pressing on both sides, force D and B outward. The vertical "diamond" becomes a horizontal diamond. The side you rolled and did not crease as you began to weave is now the front of the basket and the asterisk is the point. Notice that the color weavers are horizontal on the front and vertical in the back. See *Diagram 7* for front view.

Now weave, one row at a time, natural (soaked) strips around the top (vertical ends) in a regular over-under pattern, overlapping the ends as in *Diagrams 8* and *9*. Notice that you are bringing two stakes together and treating them as one, except at both corners. Here, you weave over or under (whatever the weaving pattern dictates) a single colored stake, as in *Diagram 10*.

Weave over and under for six rows, as in *Diagram 11*.

Finishing The Basket

Cut off inside stakes even with the top of the weaving and shape the outside stakes to a point so they can be tucked into the weaving on the inside of the basket. Rewet the outside stakes, if necessary. See *Diagram 12*.

As in *Diagram 13*, place a soaked piece of ½" flat reed around the rim, covering the top or last row of weaving on the inside and the outside, placing the overlaps near each other, with a piece of #5 round reed or seagrass in between. Hold all the pieces together with clothespins. Begin lashing as in *Diagram 14*, losing the lasher inside the rim pieces. Lash in only one direction, as in *Diagram 14*, or in both directions, forming an X as in *Diagram 15*.

Making The Handle

Cut a piece of ⅜" flat reed, 29" long. Push the ends through an opening on the sides of the basket (under the rim) and bring the ends back up about 2½" to form a loop. See *Diagram 15*. Wrap the entire handle by sticking the end of a soaked piece of ¼" flat reed between the overlapped pieces. Wrap tightly all the way across and finish in the same manner.

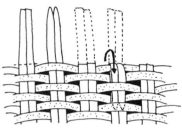

Diagram 12

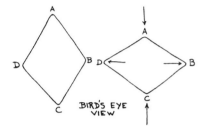

Diagram 6

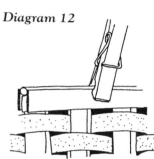

Diagram 10

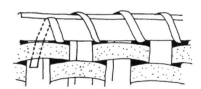

Diagram 13

FRONT VIEW

Diagram 7

Diagram 11

Diagram 14

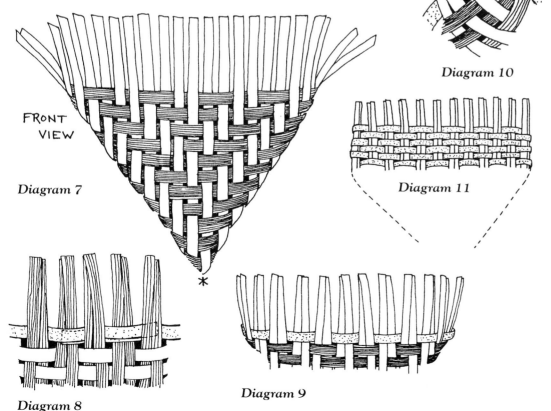

Diagram 8

Diagram 9

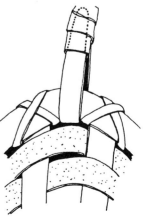

Diagram 15

3. BASKETS WITH SPECIFIC USES

carolynkerrio

*... A request for a picnic basket wasn't unusual ...
or a basket to hold kindlin' or wool.
Most people knew exactly what they wanted and how they wanted
it made, as they were for very specific uses.*

*But other times she had the freedom to make her own patterns.
Those were the most fun.
When an idea struck, she worked furiously ... yet painstakingly ...
like a Van Gogh of wood...*

TWO-PIE BASKET

TWO-PIE BASKET

This basket is a real favorite. It can serve so many purposes. Called a Two-Pie, because it is a size that will indeed hold two pies. Great for magazines, too. If you would like a shallow version of it, see measurements in parentheses following regular measurements.

Finished Size

10″ x 18″ x 14″, approximate

Materials

One 10″ x 14″ D handle
¾″ flat reed (stakes)
½″ flat reed (weavers)
One piece of ½″ flat reed, dyed blue, long enough to go around basket two times
One piece of ¼″ flat reed, dyed red, long enough to around basket one time
⅝″ flat oval reed (rim)
#6 round reed or seagrass (rim filler)
¼″ flat reed (lashing)

Cutting Stakes And Weaving The Base

From the ¾″ flat reed, cut nine pieces 36″ (29″) long and 14 pieces 27″ (20″) long. On the wrong (rougher) side, make a pencil mark at the halfway point on all the pieces. Soak all 23 pieces in cool water 2-3 minutes. Make a pencil mark on the handle at its center point as well.

Lay five of the 36″ pieces horizontally on a table in front of you, wrong side up, with center marks aligned. Then place the D handle across them on top of the center marks, making sure the center stake is in line with the center mark on the handle. See **Diagram 1**.

Next, lay the other four 36″ stakes across the D handle, in the same direction as the first five, in the spaces between the first five. See **Diagram 2**.

NOTE: If all this is too much to hold in place, lay a heavy book on one end of the stakes while you weave in some of the vertical stakes.

Consulting **Diagram 3**, weave the 14 27″ stakes, in a plain over-under pattern. There will be seven on each side of the handle. **Diagram 3** shows only one side of the handle woven. The other side should be exactly the same.

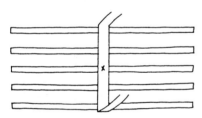

Diagram 1

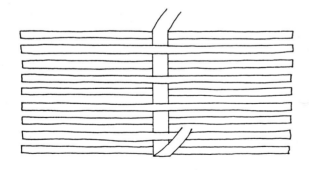

Diagram 2

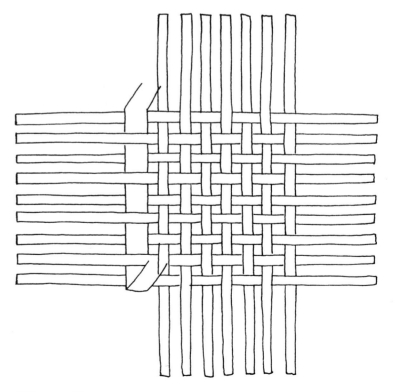

Diagram 3

Upsetting The Stakes And Weaving The Sides

Upsett all the stakes by turning them over upon themselves as in **Diagram 4**. They won't stay upright, but the crease in the stake must be made.

Begin weaving by standing the stake just past the handle (it originates from underneath the woven base) and placing the end of the weaver on top of it. See **Diagram 5**. Continue to weave in the over and under pattern all the way around the basket. When the weaver reaches its starting point, overlap four stakes (right over the beginning of the weaver) and cut it on top of the fourth stake. See **Diagram 6**.

NOTE: Treat the handle as another stake. Also note that the corners are not "squared," but rather round gently.

Weave four rows, one at a time, in this manner.

Row 5 — woven the same, but with the blue reed
Row 6 — woven the same, but with the ¼" red reed
Row 7 — woven the same, but with the blue reed (See **Diagram 7**)
Rows 8-12 — woven in natural, as the first four rows.

Finishing And Applying Rim

Cut off inside stakes even with the top of the weaving and shape the outside stakes to a point so they can be inserted into the weaving on the inside of the basket. You want to have enough length to push the end of the stake down to the third weaver or farther. See **Diagram 8**.

When all the outside stakes are inserted, wrap a soaked piece of the ⅝" flat oval reed all the way around the outside top edge of the basket, overlapping the ends about 2". Shave some of the thickness off the bottom piece. Hold this reed in place with clothespins. Then wrap another piece of the ⅝" flat oval reed around the inside top edge of the basket, overlapping the ends as before. Hold the two pieces with the same clothespins. Insert the piece of #6 round reed or seagrass on top of the rim, between the two pieces of flat oval reed, letting the ends overlap for the moment.

With a long strip of ¼" flat reed, begin to lash all the rim pieces together, as in **Diagram 9**. Use the awl to open up the space for lashing, just underneath the rim, if necessary. Lose the end of the lasher in the rim.

NOTE: If you choose to make the shallow version, you can weave two rows of natural, the three rows of color, and two more rows of natural, or you might want to use ¼" flat for all three rows of color. Rely on your own imagination to decide what colors to use and where to use them.

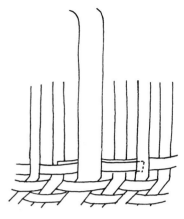

Diagram 6

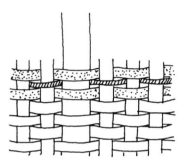

Diagram 7

Diagram 8

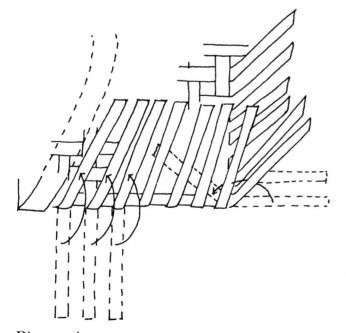

Diagram 4

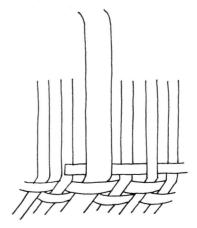

Diagram 5

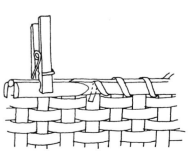

Diagram 9

RIBBED HEARTH BASKET

We all owe thanks for these instructions to Anne Boyd of Reidsville, North Carolina. The only picture I have ever seen of an old basket like this one is in Gloria Roth Teleki's book, *Collecting Traditional American Basketry.*

Finished Size

24" x 13" x 13", approximate

Materials

One Hearth frame
   (3-piece)
#7 round reed or ⅜"
   oval reed (ribs)
¼" flat reed (weavers)
Narrow cane (handle braid)

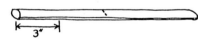

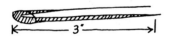

Diagram 1

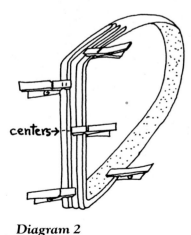

Diagram 2

The splint woven hearth has become quite familiar, but this one is ribbed. Although these instructions call for a God's Eye, try using a regular three-point lashing or a braided God's Eye. The ribs for this basket need to be pre-formed around the frame. Before putting the three frame pieces together, cut the ribs according to the directions, soak them, and clip them to the frame as directed. Allow them to dry before beginning the basket.

Cutting The Ribs

Cut two each of the following ribs from the #7 round reed or ⅜" oval reed. As you cut, number each rib near an end, but not so close the numbers will disappear with sharpening.

#1 - 28"	#5 - 24½"
#2 - 33"	#6 - 27"
#3 - 28"	#7 - 23½"
#4 - 30½"	

If you are using oval reed, sharpen the ends for 3". Mark the center on all the ribs. See *Diagram 1*.

Mark a center (as close to a center as you can) on the bottom of the D handle and in the middle of the two rims. Soak all the ribs thoroughly, for 30 minutes or so. Clamp the #6 and #7 ribs to the bottom of the D handle with clothespins. See *Diagram 2*.

Pin all the other ribs to the rim pieces, aligning the center marks. See *Diagram 3*. Allow them to dry thoroughly.

Assembling The Frame

The frames will usually come in three pieces — the D handle and the two U-shaped rim pieces. The rim pieces are angled in such a way that there are hardly any options for putting them together. Hold them in place (that may require more than two hands), with the angled ends together as in *Diagram 4*. The point of the two ends will be about three quarters of the way up the handle. Outline the rims so you can go back later and nail them in place. (Sometimes I staple them in place before nailing.) The outside ends of the U-shaped rim should be slightly touching the table.

Making The God's Eye And Inserting Ribs

Number the frame pieces as in *Diagram 6*. Soak a long ¼" flat weaver. Begin your 4-point lashing or God's Eye by placing one end of the weaver (right side out) as shown in *Diagram 6*. It moves behind 1, diagonally to 2, behind 2, diagonally to 3, behind 3, diagonally to 4, behind 4, and diagonally back to 1. You have made one complete revolution, as shown in *Diagram 7*.

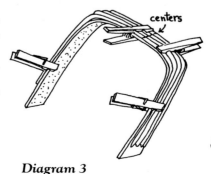

Diagram 3

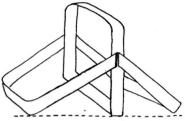

Diagram 4

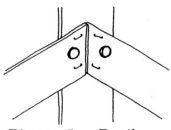

Diagram 5   *Detail*

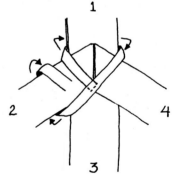

Diagram 6

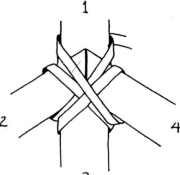

Diagram 7

RIBBED HEARTH BASKET

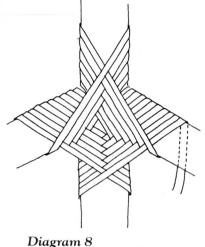

Diagram 8

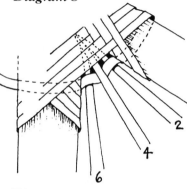

Diagram 9

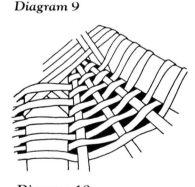

Diagram 10

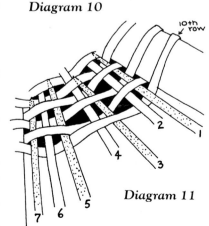

Diagram 11

Make five more revolutions, counting from the back. NOTE: Because of the severe angle of the hoops, it is inevitable that the weavers pile up in the narrow space where the frame slants downward. Do not let any of the other rows overlap; just lay them side by side. See **Diagram 8** for a finished God's Eye. **Do not cut weaver.**

Using a pencil sharpener or sharp knife, point all the ribs. Remember that the oval reed needs to be sharpened with a knife and tapered for about 3″. Be careful to sharpen without shortening.

Insert rib #2 directly under the rim, fitting each end into the "pockets" that are formed in the God's Eye. Next, insert ribs #4 and #6 below #2, as in **Diagram 9**.

Weaving And Adding More Ribs

Make sure your weaver is still damp and begin weaving as in **Diagram 9**. Treat the handle hoop as a rib. Continue to the other rim, reverse directions, and continue weaving alternately from the other row. Weave about ten rows on both sides. See **Diagram 10**.

When a weaver runs out, add a new one by overlapping the end of the old weaver and the end of the new (soaked) one, hiding the ends under a rib.

Add secondary ribs at this point. Sharpen ends (if you haven't) and insert #1 into the weaving above #2, hiding ends behind a weaver (on both sides). Insert #3 above #4, and #5 above #6. Insert #7 between #6 and the handle. See **Diagram 11**.

Continue weaving for four rows over all seven ribs. You may notice that on the first row, the weaving is "off pattern." This will correct itself on the next row, unless you have woven over two ribs somewhere. Keep the ribs as flat as you can (on the sides) by putting pressure on them as you weave. Add more ribs if you need them.

Finishing

Select a long weaver. Soak and fold it in half around the rim in the center of one end. See **Diagram 12**. Weave with both ends of the weaver, alternating each side, to the other rim. Turn around the other rim and reverse directions. Continue weaving, adding weavers as necessary, with the center strip "growing" outward toward the ears. Try to keep the sides spaced equally. Use clothespins to hold ribs in place.

Periodically, stop and press down on the handle to flatten the bottom of the basket, and at the same time, with the other hand, adjust the positions of the ribs so they are equally spaced. See **Diagram 13**. You may need to go back and tighten the weavers after you have woven some. Continue weaving and pressing until the center strip reaches the corners or "curve." When that happens, return to the other woven area and continue weaving there, outward from the ears, on both sides. The area on the "curve" or "corner" must be filled in by one of the "filling in" techniques discussed in several other instructions or in Helpful Hint #26.

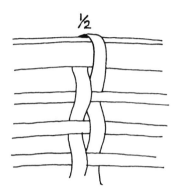

Diagram 12

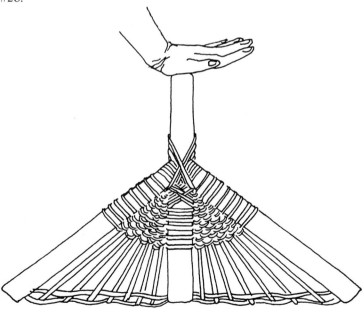

Diagram 13

FEATHER BASKET

This unusual square-to-round, lidded basket seems, historically, to have been used, as its name implies, for gathering feathers. The top, which cannot be removed, could be raised and lowered quickly to keep the feathers from blowing away.

Finished Size

12″ x 12″ x 18″

Materials

⅞″ flat reed (stakes)
⅜″ flat reed (weavers)
12″ U handle
½″ flat oval reed (rim)
3/16″ flat reed (lashing and weavers)
Approx. 3′ #6 round reed (rim)
Approx. 8′ #4 round reed (twining around lid)
12″ x 7/16″ carnival hoop (shaping device)

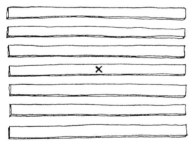

Diagram 1

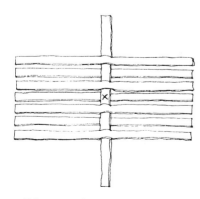

Diagram 2

Most basket historians seem to agree that the basket probably served other purposes as well, perhaps as a lunch pail or shopping basket. It is not one of the easiest baskets to construct, but rewarding in the end if you persist.

Cutting Stakes And Weaving The Bottom

Cut 14 pieces of the ⅞″ flat reed 30″ long. Pencil mark the centers of two of these pieces with an "X" on the wrong side (wrong side is the rougher side).

Soak all 14 pieces of reed for a minute or two in cool water. Place seven of the soaked stakes horizontally, wrong side up, making sure the fourth or middle stake has its center marked. The stakes should be approximately ¼″ apart. See *Diagram 1*.

Once these seven stakes are in place, weave the other stake with its center marked, perpendicularly, over and under the other center. Be sure to match the two center marks. See *Diagram 2*.

Now weave the other six stakes over and under, three on each side of the middle stake, making sure the weaving is alternating on each row. You have now formed the bottom of the basket. With a tape measure or yardstick, measure from side to side at several points to be sure the bottom is square — it should be 8″ square. See *Diagram 3*.

Upsetting The Sides

To upsett the sides of the basket, bend and press each stake all the way over on itself to form a permanent crease at the base of the stake. You may want to use a flat ruler or piece of flat reed placed on the bottom of the stakes as a guide.

Press the stakes over the ruler in the direction of the woven bottom. See *Diagram 4*.

The stake will return itself to an approximate upright position. Continue all the way around.

Weaving The Sides

Soak one long strip of the ⅜″ flat reed (weaver) for a couple of minutes. If you have made other market-style baskets, you upsett the sides, and made a concentrated effort on the first row of weaving to make the stakes stand absolutely upright. This basket does not have straight sides; rather, they flare out gradually and the corners "round," beginning with the very first row. It is important that you concentrate on rounding the corners, especially on the first and second rows of weaving. Once the form is established, the weaving will, for the most part, fall into place.

When you look at the woven bottom of the basket, notice that some of the stakes originate underneath the weaving and some originate on top. Begin weaving (with the wet weaver you soaked) by placing the end behind one of the stakes that originates on the top of the weaving. Weave with the right side of the reed on the outside of the basket. This way you are making the bottom stakes (the ones that originate from underneath) stand upright first. The next row of weaving will pick up the other stakes. Instead of trying to make the stakes stand upright, allow them to lean outward (as is their natural tendency), and do not pinch or square the corners. (You may go back later and tighten if the weaving is too loose.) See *Diagram 5*.

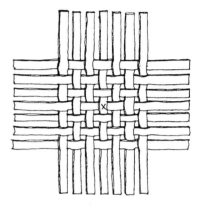

Diagram 3

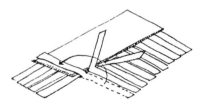

Diagram 4

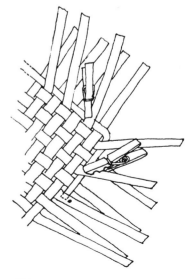

Diagram 5

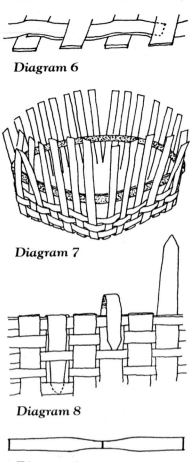

Diagram 6

Diagram 7

Diagram 8

Diagram 9

Diagram 10

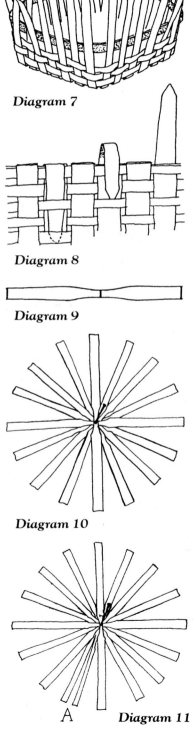

Diagram 11

When you have woven over and under all the way around the basket, and are back to where you began, allow about 2″ to overlap the starting point and cut the weaver. Hide the ends of the weavers behind a stake. The end of a weaver need never show from the inside or the outside. See *Diagram 6*.

Begin weaving the next row, and each row thereafter, in a different place so as not to get a build-up from constantly starting and stopping in the same place.

When you have woven three rows, place a 12″ hoop inside the stakes and clothespin it every 3″ or 4″ to the stakes. It should remain in the basket about 4″ above the weaving until you are ready to finish off the rim. Move the hoop up a little as you weave; this will give you a guide to follow and will aid in the "rounding" process. See *Diagram 7*. Weave to within 3″ of tops of stakes.

Finishing The Tops Of Stakes

NOTE: You can leave the 12″ hoop inside the basket and finish off the rim over the hoop if you desire. It certainly adds stability to the basket to do so, but it is quite sturdy with only the ½″ flat oval around the rim.

When you have finished weaving, you will find that half your stakes are behind the last weaver and half are in front of it. Wet the top part of the stakes again. With scissors or wire cutters, cut off the inside stakes even with the last row of weaving. Then with scissors or wire cutters, shape the outside stakes to a point. Bend the pointed stakes over and insert them into the weaving inside the basket, making sure they reach at least behind the third row of weaving if not farther. See *Diagram 8*.

Set the basket aside at this point and construct the lid. The handle is inserted only after the lid is made and fitted to the top of the basket. The handle is inserted through the lid, allowing the lid to be raised but not removed.

Making The Lid: Cutting And Placing The Stakes

From the ⅞″ flat reed, cut seven strips, 18″ long. Mark the centers of all these pieces with a pencil on the wrong side (rougher side).

With scissors, taper both sides of all seven strips for about 3″ on each side of the center mark, so that it is about ⅜″ at the center. See *Diagram 9*.

Place all seven of the strips, each on top of the other, until they look like spokes in a wheel. Space them as evenly as possible. These spokes may be either nailed down to a wooden surface, placed on a T-pin, or they can simply be held in place with one hand while you begin to weave with the other. See *Diagram 10*.

Beginning To Weave

With scissors, split any one of the 14 spokes in half. This split spoke will be referred to as "A." You now have 15 spokes. See *Diagram 11*.

Now take a ¼″ or 3/16″ weaver that is approximately 4′ in length. With scissors, begin cutting it in half lengthwise. For about 3′ the weaver will be about ⅛″ wide. After approximately 3′, begin to taper the width, making the weaver wider and wider until it reaches its normal width. Coil the weaver and soak 1 to 3 minutes.

Remove from water and insert the end of the ⅛″ weaver between the two pieces of "A" and begin to weave over and under each spoke all the way around the circle of spokes. See *Diagram 12*.

NOTE: You will find that you must start the weaving about 2″ out from the center. You want to be sure the first row is snug, but if you try to force this first row too close to the center, the second row will not fit. Weave five rows around and stop at the second spoke before "A." See *Diagram 13*.

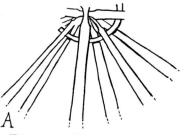

Diagram 12

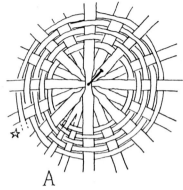

Diagram 13

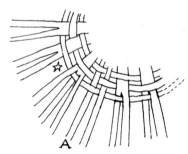

Diagram 14

Diagram 15

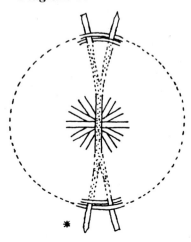

Diagram 16

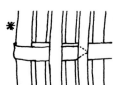

Diagram 16 A

FEATHER BASKET

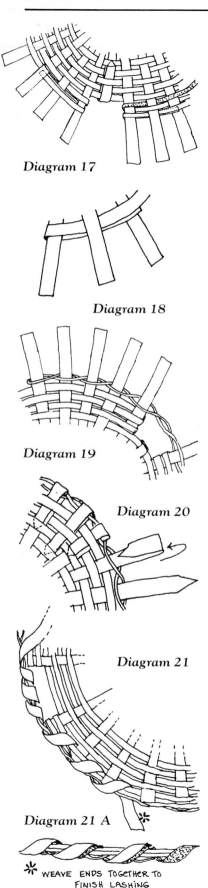

Diagram 17

Diagram 18

Diagram 19

Diagram 20

Diagram 21

Diagram 21 A

※ WEAVE ENDS TOGETHER TO FINISH LASHING

Splitting The Spokes

When you have woven five or six rows, find the spoke immediately before "A." With scissors, cut this spoke into three equal parts. Then cut all remaining spokes in half. See *Diagram 14*. Then continue to weave over and under each new spoke, beginning with the spoke you cut into 3 equal parts.

NOTE: As you weave this flat area, you will need to spread the stakes apart, spacing them as evenly as you can. Make sure your woven area is staying round. If it isn't, use an awl to push areas in or pull them out to keep it round. You must also make every effort to keep the lid flat. There will be a natural tendency for the edges to curl up. Sometimes placing a heavy book on the woven area after about 6" will help to keep it flat. It doesn't seem to be too objectionable if the center rises a little, which often happens, as it prevents the edge from curling so much.

Splicing On A New Weaver

When you see that you have only 2" or 3" of the weaver remaining, it is time to splice on a new weaver. This is achieved by laying a new ¼" weaver on top of the 2" of the old weaver you have left and hiding the end under a spoke. Continue to weave with the two weavers together until the old one runs out. Then continue with the new one. Just don't exert a great deal of pressure on the new weaver until you have finished a complete revolution. See *Diagram 15*.

Finishing The Top

Weave in this manner until the lid measures 11½" **or** is within ½" of fitting your basket's top. You have two more rows to weave at this point, leaving a space for the handle to be inserted, so check the size closely. If the top of your basket, by some chance, is smaller or larger than 12", you must adjust the lid size accordingly.

When your weaving is within ½" of the basket size, select one spoke that runs from one side to the other. (From the one original spoke, there are now 4, since they were split.) Select the one spoke on each side that is on top of the weaving, taper the ends and tuck them into the weaving on the wrong side. Eliminating this spoke from the weaving creates the space for the handle. See *Diagrams 16* and **16A**.

Continue with the weaving until you reach the spoke you tucked under. Reverse directions around the spoke before it, weave back around to the other tucked in spoke. Reverse again. Return to the point at which you first reversed. Make the final turn, and cut the weaver so that the end hides behind a spoke. See *Diagram 17*.

Begin a new weaver by wrapping it around the first spoke on the other side, leaving enough free to tuck under itself. See *Diagram 18*. Weave two rows between this point and the other side, cut and tuck the end under as before.

Finally, using the well-soaked #4 round reed and beginning anywhere before the openings, fold it in half and twine all the way around the edge. When you reach the openings, make two twists and continue twining around each spoke. Tuck the ends into the weaving any way it is convenient. See *Diagram 19*.

Point all the spokes and tuck them into the weaving on the wrong side (inside of lid). See *Diagram 20*. With ⅜" flat reed, lash around the lid as in *Diagrams 21* and **21A**.

Inserting The Handle

Insert the handle through the openings on the lid. Locate two center stakes on the basket, directly across from each other, (preferably the ones that were cut flush with the top of the basket), and insert the handle into the weaving on the inside. The handle can be inserted into the weaving as far as it needs to give the desired height. Nail, glue, or staple it in place. A small tack through the handle and the top weaver works well. See *Diagram 22*. (A lock handle also works and eliminates the need for nailing.)

Applying The Rim

With all the outside stakes pushed down into the weaving and the handle in place, lift up the lid as far as it will go (hold in place with clothespins if necessary) and wrap a piece of ½" flat oval reed all the way around the outside, overlapping the ends about 3", and hold in place with clothespins. Then wrap a piece of ½" flat oval reed all around the inside, overlapping the ends as before. Hold both pieces in place with the same clothespins.

Lastly, put a piece of #6 round reed between the two pieces of flat oval, allowing the ends to overlap a little for the moment. See *Diagram 23*. Be sure to bevel or thin the ends of the flat oval so the overlapped area is the regular thickness of the reed.

Lashing The Rim

With a long strip of 3/16" flat reed, begin to lash all the rim pieces together, as in *Diagram 24*. Use an awl, if necessary, to open the space for lashing. When you are within 1" of finishing, cut the piece of round reed so the ends butt against each other and finish by tucking the ends of the lashing weaver into the weaving discreetly.

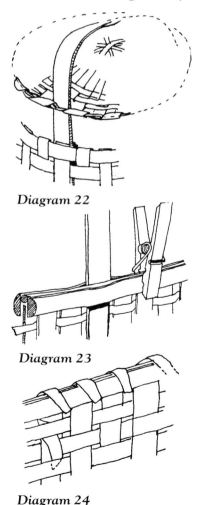

Diagram 22

Diagram 23

Diagram 24

DOUBLE LIDDED PICNIC BASKET

There are several means of attaching a lid to any ribbed basket. The technique used here is unique in that there is a woven bar instead of the one or two dowels often used.

Finished Size

20″ x 12″ x 20″

Materials

Two 12″ x 20″ oval hoops (frame)
3/16″ or ¼″ reed (weavers)
⅜″ oval or #7 round reed (ribs)
#10 round reed (lid frame)
3/16″ or 11/64″ flat reed (handle trim)

I owe this technique to a very special basket-maker friend, Kristen Aymar, who found an old basket made this way, disassembled it to learn just how it was made, and shared her knowledge with me. The lid can be used on any shape ribbed basket. It just happens that the 12″ x 20″ ovals produce a nice size picnic basket.

Positioning Hoops And Constructing Bar For Lid

Place the two 12″ x 20″ oval hoops together as in **Diagram 1**. Hold them in place temporarily with clothespins or tie with waxed string. Adjust the position of the hoops, while measuring with a tape measure from one side to the other, until the distance is equal on all four sides. Make a pencil mark on both hoops, on all four sides, at the intersecting points. See **Diagram 1A**.

Separate the hoops and prepare the #10 round reed for the bar. Since the two oval hoops are the same, you may use either for the exposed handle.

Cut a piece of #10 round reed 30″ long, or the length required to form the bar in **Diagram 3**. Shave about half the thickness off the reed from approximately 4″ on one end with a knife or shaper. Shave half the thickness from the opposite side of the other end of the reed. NOTE: The two ends will overlap and should be about the same thickness as the whole #10 round reed when spliced together. Using **Diagram 2** as a guide, scoop out a 1″ area approximately 13″ from one end and 16″

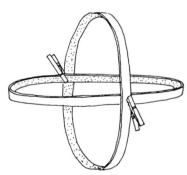

Diagram 1

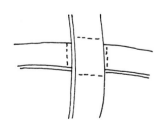

Diagram 1 A

Diagram 2

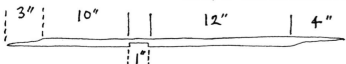

from the other end. This area wraps around the handle and should be thinned to about half its thickness.

Soak the shaped #10 round reed thoroughly (at least 30 minutes). Fit the bar around the handle hoop, just above the pencil mark you made across the rim hoop. See **Diagram 3**. Hold the bar in place with clips, string, or nails.

Weaving The Bar

Soak the longest ¼″ flat or flat-oval reed you can find. When it is pliable, begin by pushing the end between the two pieces of the bar where they are spliced, about 1½″ from the handle. Wrap around the two pieces of the splice moving toward the handle. See **Diagram 4**. When you reach the handle, begin to weave, figure eight style, around the two sides of the bar. Fit the first row as close as possible to the handle. See **Diagram 5**. When you have woven to the other handle, hide the end by pushing it back into the weaving or down behind the bar as it wraps around the hoop (on the outside).

NOTE: Take care to weave the bar with even tension so the width of the bar will remain consistent. If time allows, let the bar dry before starting to weave.

NOTE: If your weaver isn't long enough to weave all the way across, add a new one by weaving with both the old one and a new (soaked) one together for about an inch, then continue with the new one alone. Cut the old one, if need be, so the end hides inside the bar or under the new weaver.

Decorating The Handle

Any decoration may be used or the handle may be left plain. If you feel the handle needs more width, consider using a piece of #7 reed

on both sides of the handle hoop and do a simple over-under weave or add the wheat braid as illustrated in the following step:

Cut two pieces of #7 round reed 2″ longer than the exposed handle. For about an inch (on all sides), shave the ends on two sides until they are about the thickness of flat reed. Push two of the pieces down

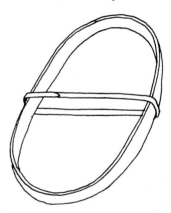

Diagram 3

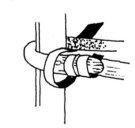

Diagram 4

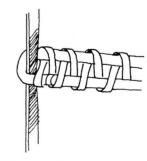

Diagram 5

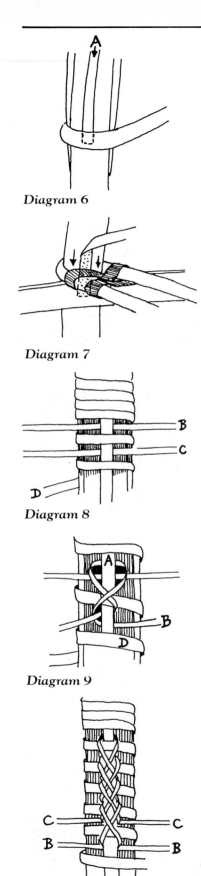

Diagram 6

Diagram 7

Diagram 8

Diagram 9

Diagram 10

between the bar and the handle hoop, one on each side of the handle. See *Diagram 6*.

Cut the following:

1. From 3/16″ flat reed, cut and soak a piece (A) approximately 5″ longer than the handle.
2. From 3/16″ flat reed, cut and soak two strips (B and C) that are three times as long as the exposed handle. Mark a half-way point on the wrong or rougher side.
3. Locate and soak a very long piece of ¼″ flat or flat oval reed (D).

Push one end of the 3/16″ flat reed (A) between the bar and the rim hoop to secure. See *Diagram 6*.

Push one end of the long weaver (D) between the two hoops on the inside. See *Diagram 7*. Begin with (D) wrapping around the handle solidly, over (A), seven or eight times. Wrap around the handle and the two pieces of #7 round reed.

Insert strip (B) under (A), aligning the halfway mark under (A), wrong side up. Make one complete revolution around the handle with (D) going over (A). See *Diagram 8*.

Insert strip (C) under (A), again aligning the center mark directly under (A), flat side up. Make another wrap with (D). At this point, your handle should look like *Diagram 8*.

NOTE: The above procedure will be easier if you will remember that following every movement with (B) and (C), the weaver (D) makes one complete turn around the handle.

Braiding

Consulting *Diagram 9*, bring the left side of (B) down and under (A), entering from the right and coming out on the left. Next, bring the right side down, entering from the left, move under (A) and under the left side of (B), bringing it out on the right side. Pull both ends of (B), tightening the figure eight. With (D), make one complete turn around the handle, over (A). Repeat the procedure with (C). Be sure to tighten and wrap with (D) after each figure eight. *Diagram 10* shows five braid crosses, with (C) to be braided next.

Alternative Weaving Of The Handle

This is basically the same handle treatment. The only difference is that instead of wrapping all the way around the handle and the round reed, you weave over one round reed, under the handle, over and around the other round reed, over the handle this time, under the round reed, etc. See *Diagram 10A*.

Making The Braided God's Eye

NOTE: The God's Eye is made right over the bar and the handle wrapping.

Referring to *Diagram 11*, start the weaver on top of the hoops, with the tail on top pointing between the rims 3 and 4. The weaver moves behind 1 and diagonally to 2, under itself, and diagonally to 3. Then behind 3, under itself and diagonally to 4, behind 4, under itself and diagonally to 1.

At this point, the procedure changes somewhat. See *Diagram 12*. The weaver will now go under itself on 1, diagonally to 2 and underneath the outermost on 2, behind 2, under itself and the outermost weaver on 3, etc. It will be necessary to use the awl to lift the second weaver up enough for the end of the weaver to slip under it. It might also be helpful to point the end of the weaver. The weaving moves from one hoop to the next, counter clockwise, always going under itself and the outermost weaver on the next hoop.

Continue weaving in this manner until you have made seven (more if you like) revolutions, counting from the back of the hoops, with the weaver ending on 4 at the top of the right rim. Now you are ready to begin weaving the basket. Do not cut the weaver. Secure it at the rim with a clothespin and begin with another soaked weaver to repeat the procedure on the other side of the basket. The finished God's Eye should look like the one in *Diagram 14*.

NOTE: Diagrams show God's Eye loosely woven for clarity.

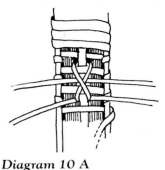

Diagram 10 A

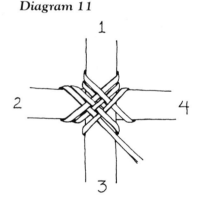

Diagram 11

Diagram 12

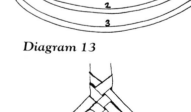

Diagram 13

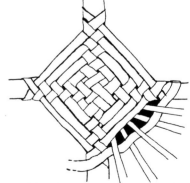

Diagram 14

DOUBLE LIDDED PICNIC BASKET

Weaving The Basket

NOTE: I have made this basket using both of the suggested materials (#7 round reed and ⅜″ oval-oval reed) and have found the oval reed to produce a sturdier basket.

From the #7 round reed (or oval reed) cut and number two each of the following lengths:

Primary Ribs

#1 - 29″	#4 - 36″
#2 - 31″	#5 - 29″
#3 - 34″	

Secondary Ribs

#6 - 28″ (inserted below #1)
#7 - 34″ (inserted below #3)
#8 - 31″ (inserted below #4)
#9 - 25½″ (inserted below #5)

With a sharp knife, shaver, or pencil sharpener, point all the rib ends as in **Diagram 13**.

Begin by placing the ribs in the God's Eye; they actually just lie inside the ear. Although **Diagram 14** shows all five primary ribs inserted when the weaving begins, you may find it much easier to begin with ribs #1, #3, and #5, weave a couple of rows and then add #2 and #4. Then weave five or six rows with the weaver left over from the God's Eye, before adding the secondary ribs in the places indicated in the length chart. See **Diagram 15**. The weave is a simple over-under, turning around the handle to reverse the weave. Rewet the weaver any time that it feels dry or stiff. Push each row of weaving as snugly as possible against the previous row. **Diagram 15** shows the weaving loose only for clarity.

After adding the secondary ribs and weaving several rows, you will find that there are still spaces between ribs which are wider than 1″. The size of the spaces will vary according to the tension each individual uses in weaving. You should add more ribs in these spaces. Estimate the length of the additional ribs by holding the reed around from one side to the other, allowing enough extra to insert into the weaving. Be sure the ribs are in keeping with the "skeleton" already formed. See **Diagram 16** for the basket's basic shape.

Diagram 15

Diagram 16

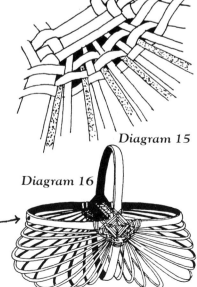

dot →

Diagram 17

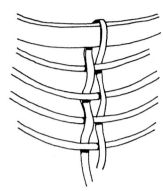

Diagram 18

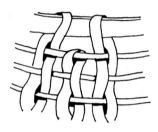

Diagram 19

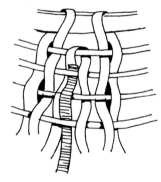

Diagram 20

Diagram 21

Splicing A New Weaver

When you have 2" or 3" of weaver left, it is time to join a new (soaked) weaver. This joining should not take place at the rim, so backtrack if necessary. Referring to **Diagram 17**, overlap the new weaver on top of the old one. You will be weaving with two pieces of reed for two or three ribs. Hide the ends if possible.

Finishing The Basket

Weave approximately the same number of rows on each side to keep the basket balanced. When you have woven (on both sides) for 5" or 6" from the ears, begin a new weaver in the middle of the unwoven area which remains. The place for this weaver to begin is marked with a "dot" in **Diagram 16**.

Fold a long soaked weaver in half over the rim. See **Diagram 18**. Use clothespins frequently to keep the ribs evenly spaced. You are now weaving with one end of the weaver at at time, in two directions — one end toward the left and one end toward the right. When this weaving covers about 5" or 6" of the rim, stop weaving here and return to the original weaving on either side. When the two areas meet, you should "fill in" the triangular unwoven space in the following manner. When you can no longer squeeze another weaver in around the rim, do one of the following:

1. Turn around the first rib, reversing direction just as you did around the rim (See **Diagram 19**), or
2. Cut the weaver inside the basket and begin a new one going in the opposite direction (See **Diagram 20**).

Making And Attaching The Lid

Measure, as accurately as possible, the distance from inside one God's Eye to the other (across the basket at the bar). Cut a piece of #10 round reed or a ¼" diameter dowel (A) the length of your measurement. Next, measure from inside one ear all the way around the rim to the outer ear. **Be sure the lid will fit on top of the rim and inside the ear.** Cut a piece (B) 6" longer than the measurement. See **Diagram 21**.

For 3" on each end, shave away at least half the thickness of the reed. Soak the #10 round reed and tie it, as it forms the shape of the rim on which it is to fit. Fold the thinned ends around the straight piece of #10 round reed while it is wet, as in **Diagram 22**, and hold it in place with cable clips or clothespins. When the frame is dry, soak a long piece of ¼" flat reed and begin weaving the lid ears as in **Diagrams 22** and **22A**.

Refer to **Diagram 22A** and insert the weaver and wrap as tightly as you can, around the splice 2 times to secure the splice. Next, refer to **Diagram 22** and begin a 2-point lashing, around bar A then around B, forming a V-shaped ear. You should have five or six wraps on each side. Repeat the procedure on the other side of the lid. Do not cut the weaver.

From #7 round reed, cut two each of the following ribs:

#1 - 15"
#2 - 17½"
#3 - 20"

Begin with three primary ribs. Rib #1 is inserted into the opening in the ear closest to the straight side, rib #3 into the opening at the bottom, and rib #2 into the center of the openings. You must create an opening with the awl. Weave over and under, just as you wove the basket, as in **Diagram 23**, for three or four rows. **Diagram 24** shows the approximate placement of the first three ribs.

Add four more ribs, as indicated in **Diagram 25**. It should be easy for you to eyeball the lengths of these ribs — you want the space between the ribs, at their fullest point, to be no wider than 1". Add more ribs, if needed, after 2" or 3" of weaving. Weave some on each side of the lid to keep the weaving balanced and the lid in shape. Again, you may want to begin a weaver in the middle of the unwoven area after about 4" of weaving from the ear. As in **Diagram 26**, the two areas to be filled in will be on the sides. Fill them in with the same techniques you used on the basket.

The lid can be attached to the bar with a piece of soaked reed pushed through the lid and around the bar and "tied" underneath. A strong waxed string, leather, or wire can also be used to join the two.

Diagram 22   Diagram 22 A

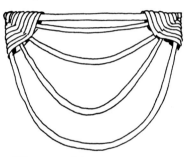

Diagram 23

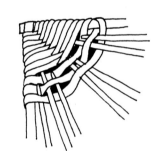

Diagram 24

Diagram 25

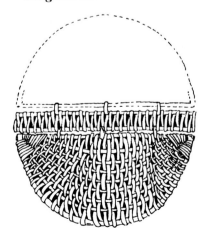

Diagram 26

WOOL DRYING BASKET

The wool drying basket was used historically for just that — drying fleece. Those that were really used for this purpose probably were not woven in a twill pattern, but rather in a plain weave so that air could circulate through the wool. They had legs for the same reason. You can make yours without legs or you can purchase legs from some suppliers if you don't wish to cut them yourself. We are indebted to Shelby Underwood and Louise Grubb for these directions.

Finished size

11″ x 11″ x 12″, approximate

Materials

⅝″ flat reed (stakes and weavers)
⅝″ flat oval reed (rim)
#6 or #7 round reed (rim filler)
4 legs (optional)
#12 spline or #12 round reed or 2 bushel basket handles (handles)

Preparing Materials And Weaving The Base

From the ⅝″ flat reed, cut 34 pieces 34″ long. Mark the centers (on the wrong side) of some of the pieces. NOTE: You can align a few center marks and from there align the ends of the stakes. Soak all the pieces until they are pliable.

Lay 17 stakes, horizontally, on a flat surface in front of you, wrong sides up. See **Diagram 1**.

Pattern Chart
(O = Over, U = Under)

Left Of A

O1, U2, O2 ending O2
U2, O2, U2 ending U1
U1, O2, U2 ending U2
O2, U2, O2 ending O1

Right Of A

U1, O2, U2 ending U2
U2, O2, U2 ending U1
O1, U2, O2 ending O2
O2, U2, O2 ending O1

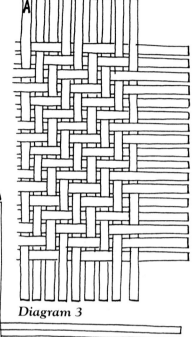

Diagram 3

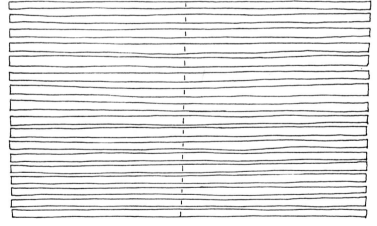

Diagram 1

Weave the center stake across the center marks as in **Diagram 2**. From the top the pattern is: Over 2, under 2, over 2, under 2, etc., and ending over 1. The center stake is labeled "A" as in **Diagram 3**. From this point follow the Pattern Chart, weaving eight stakes to the right of "A" and eight stakes to the left. See **Diagram 3**.

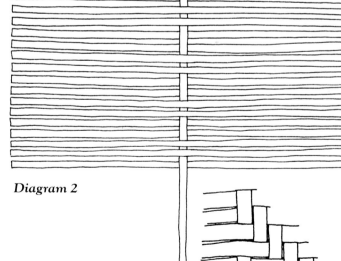

Diagram 2

Repeat the pattern twice on both sides. Pack the stakes tightly together. Measure and true the base to 11″ square, marking the corners. See **Diagram 4**.

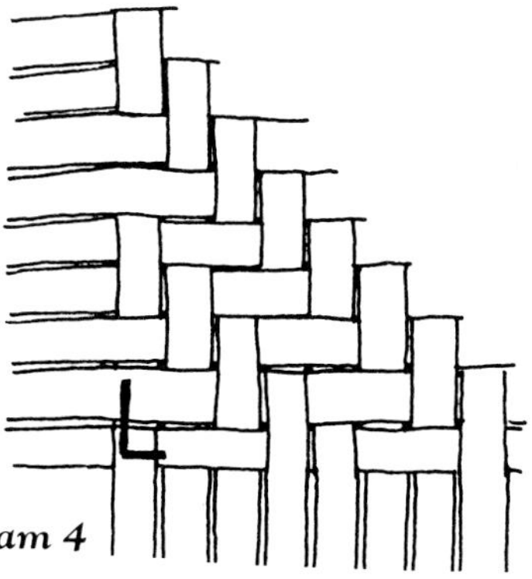

Diagram 4

WOOL DRYING BASKET

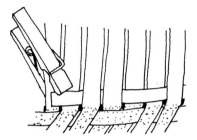

Diagram 5

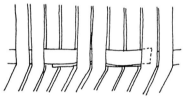

Diagram 6

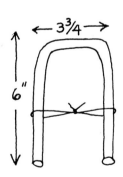

Diagram 7

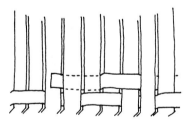

Diagram 8

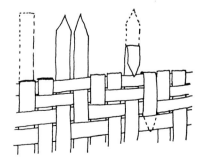

Diagram 9

Weaving The Sides

Upsett all the stakes by bending each one over upon itself (toward the base) to form a permanent crease at the base of the stakes. See **Diagram 5**.

Begin weaving with a long, soaked piece of ⅝" flat reed by going around any two stakes. Hold the weaver in place with clothespins or a brake. Continue under 2, over 2 all the way around the basket. See **Diagram 6**. End the row by overlapping the beginning end for six stakes to secure the weaver and hide the end. See **Diagram 7**.

Start another row (on a different side) by going over the second of the stakes that was outside on the first row and continuing over 2, under 2 around the basket again. You have "stepped up" one stake. See **Diagram 8**.

Weave in the same manner for twelve rows. Do not square the corners; let them "round" and the top will be round or oval. Pack all the rows down as snugly as possible.

Point all the outside stakes and cut the inside ones flush with the top row of weaving. See **Diagram 9**. Tuck the pointed ones into the weaving inside the basket.

Finishing

If you have bushel basket handles, insert them into two opposite sides, centering them in the weaving. If you are making your own handles, refer to the "loop" directions in the Shaker Cat-Head or Cherokee Picnic Basket instructions. See **Diagrams 10** and **11** for dimensions of handles and **Diagram 12** for insertion.

Soak enough ⅝" flat oval reed to go around the top of the basket two times plus 6" - 8" for overlap. Bevel, or scarf, the ends of the two pieces as in **Diagram 13**. Place one piece on the inside and one on the outside. Hold them in place with clothespins or cable clips. Next, fit a piece of #7 round reed around the top of the basket above the two rim pieces. Scarf the ends of it as well.

Begin a lasher by pushing one end down between the two rim pieces. Wrap around the round reed as many times as are needed to reach the second stake. See **Diagram 14**. Take the lasher straight down into the space between the stakes, under the rim, to emerge on the other side and wrap again around the round reed. End the lashing by losing it between the rim pieces. Scarf the other end of the round reed so the two ends fit together smoothly and can be wrapped.

Insert the legs as in **Diagram 15**. They usually fit snugly, but in case they don't, nail them to a weaver or the rim, if they reach. Place two on one side, with the end stakes, and two on the opposite side with the same stakes.

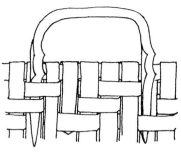

Diagram 12

Diagram 13

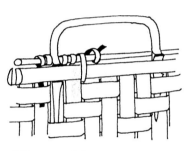

Diagram 14

← 3¾ →

6"

Diagram 10

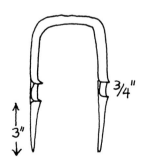

¾"

3"

Diagram 11

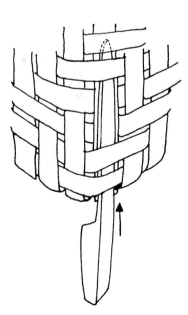

Diagram 15

WINE BASKET

The wine basket is made to hold two bottles of wine, or two bottles of anything that fits. The divider in the center of the basket keeps the two bottles separated. It is great for a picnic or for long stemmed flowers. Color it, add decorative strips, or just leave it plain.

Finished Size

4½″ x 9″ x 14″, approximate

Materials

4½″ x 14″ basket handle (handle)
½″ flat reed (stakes)
⅜″ flat reed (weavers)
½″ flat-oval reed (rim)
#6 round reed (rim)
3/16″ flat reed (lashing & divider)

Cutting Stakes And Weaving The Bottom

Begin by marking a center on the bottom (topside) of the handle. From the ½″ flat reed, cut 8 strips 27″ long and 5 strips 34″ long. From the ⅜″ flat reed, cut 4 strips 15″ long. Mark the centers of all the pieces on the wrong (rough) side. Soak them all in cool water for 2-3 minutes.

Begin by laying three of the 34″ strips horizontally on the table in front of you, wrong side up, making the two outside pieces fit the width of the handle (about 4½″). Place the handle on top of the three strips, aligned with the center marks of all the strips. See *Diagram 1*.

Align the center of the middle stake with the center mark on the handle bottom. Place the other 34″ strips on top of the handle, spacing them evenly. Then lay the 15″ strips on either side of the two longer strips with center marks aligned. While weaving the bottom, treat the long strip and the short strip on either side as one stake. See *Diagram 2*.

Weave the bottom with the 27″ pieces in a basic over and under pattern. The first row, closest to the handle, should weave under the first stake, over the next 3, under 1, over 3 and under 1. The next row is woven opposite the first (over the first stake, under 3, etc.). Repeat these two pattern rows with all the remaining 27″ strips, four rows on each side of the handle. When all the rows are woven, measure and true the base to approximately 4½″ x 9″. See *Diagram 3*.

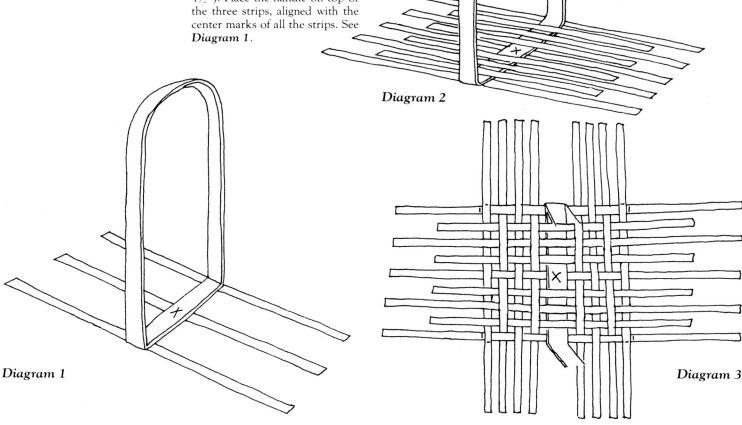

Diagram 1

Diagram 2

Diagram 3

WINE BASKET

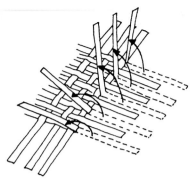

Diagram 4

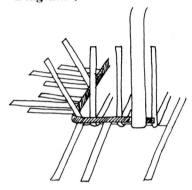

Diagram 5

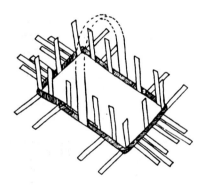

Diagram 6

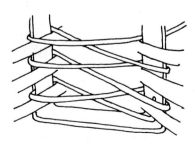

Diagram 7

Upsetting The Stakes And Weaving The Sides

Upsett the stakes by bending each stake over upon itself toward the woven base, forming a permanent crease at the base of the stake. See **Diagram 4**. The stakes will not remain upright until two rows of weaving are done.

Begin weaving with a soaked piece of ⅜″ flat reed by placing the end on the outside of the stake to the right or left of the handle, depending on which direction you prefer to weave. The wrong side of the reed should be toward the inside of the basket.

NOTE: By beginning at this point, you will be making the stakes that originate from underneath the woven mat stand up first. They are anchored by a horizontal stake. See **Diagram 5**. For a while, ignore the short filler strips. Leave them lying down and deal only with the long stakes.

When you have woven all the way around the basket, end by going over the first four stakes you wove. Cut the weaver behind the fourth stake. Consult **Diagram 6** to see that both ends will be hidden either behind a stake or a weaver.

Weaving The Divider

Once the first two rows are woven, begin the divider (a long piece of soaked, 3/16″ flat reed) by tucking one end under a ⅜″ weaver as it goes around the handle on the inside of the basket. It then begins a figure eight pattern by moving to the other side of the handle and around the outside. NOTE: The divider is hidden on the outside of the handle underneath the ⅜″ weavers.

Continue the figure eight all the way up as you weave the sides of the basket and finish it by securing the end under the last row of weaving just as you began. Be sure the divider strip is securely fastened even if you must make a complete turn around the last weaver. See **Diagram 7**.

At any point, after you have woven four rows around the basket, you can point the ends of the four filler strips and tuck them under the fourth row of weaving. Allow the ends to lean inward to form a point, under row four. See **Diagram 8**. Weave a total of 16 rows if you use all ⅜″ flat.

Finishing The Top And Lashing

Finish the tops of the stakes by cutting the inside stakes flush with the last row of weaving and pointing the outside stakes to a length that can be tucked into the weaving inside the basket, thereby hiding all the ends. Dampen the ends before bending if they are dry. See **Diagram 9**.

After finishing the stakes, place a soaked piece of ½″ flat oval reed around the inside top of the basket, covering the top row of weaving. Bevel the ends for an inch or two with a knife or shaper and allow them to overlap as far as they are beveled. See **Diagram 10**.

Hold the flat oval reed in place with clothespins. Next, follow the same procedures with the flat oval reed on the outside of the basket. Hold both pieces in place with the same clothespins. Then place the #6 round reed between and on top of the two pieces of ½″ flat oval reed, still using the same clothespins to secure all the reeds. Cut the piece of #6 round reed 1″ - 2″ too long so that it can be cut to fit later. See **Diagram 11**.

Begin lashing with the soaked 3/16″ flat reed by bringing the end up between the two pieces of flat oval and moving over and under the rim pieces, from one hole to the next. When you have lashed all the way around the basket, end the weaver by the same means you began: Bring the end of the lashing weaver up between the two rim pieces and cut off flush with the top. Make the ends of the #6 round "butt" together. If you wish, you çan begin another piece of weaver and lash in the opposite direction, forming an "X" on the rim and the handle. See **Diagram 12**.

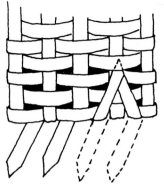

Diagram 8

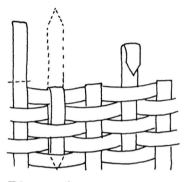

Diagram 9

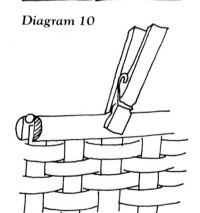

Diagram 10

Diagram 11

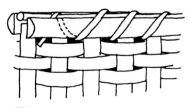

Diagram 12

CHEROKEE PICNIC BASKET

The basic design of this basket is borrowed from the Cherokee Indians. They typically use dyed weavers, which you may use as well. For interest, you can vary the widths of weavers. One very wide 2″ - 3″ strip of poplar can be used for your own painting or stenciling.

Finished Size

11″ x 15″ x 12″, approximate

Materials

1″ flat reed (stakes)
⅝″ flat reed (weavers)
¼″ flat reed (weavers)
½″ flat reed (fillers - 5 yds.)
½″ flat-oval reed (rim - 3 yds.)
Swing handles or #14 round reed
#12 spline or #12 round reed (loops)
One 10″ x 10″ square hoop (for shaping handles)
8′ #5 or #6 round reed (rims)

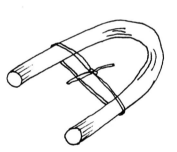

Diagram 1

If you do not have access to swing handles, they can be made with #14 round reed, for which directions are given. Be adventurous and experiment with your own choice of reed sizes and lengths. Some illustrations show the swing handle, others the handmade, threaded swing handle.

Making The Loops And Handles

Loops: From the #12 round reed or spline, cut four pieces 10″ long and soak them thoroughly (at least one hour). After they are well-soaked and pliable, bend them gently to form a very "skinny" U shape (1″ to 1½″ wide). Secure the shape by tying or placing a heavy rubber band around each piece. They must dry in shape, for later use. See *Diagram 1*.

Handles: To make your own swing handles, cut two pieces of #14 round reed approximately 40″ long. Because round reed twists so easily, make a pencil mark all the way down one side following the grain. You will do most of your shaving from this side and can be sure that the reed has not twisted or turned. See *Diagram 2*.

Make a mark at 20″ (center) across the reed; measure 9″ from each end. With a sharp knife or shaper, taper each end according to *Diagram 3*. The first 4″ should be rounded and about 3/16″ in diameter at the end. From 4″ to 9″, the reed should gradually become larger and flatter, shaving from the side with the straight grain mark and the opposite side. See *Diagram 3A*. When you are satisfied with the shaping, sand the area well, especially at the 9″ mark, so it smoothly becomes round again. Place the whole strip in water for several hours.

You need a form around which to shape the handle — a 10″ x 10″ square market rim (hoop) works well. If you prefer a rounded handle, use a 10″ round hoop. Make a mark on one side of the 10″ x 10″ as nearly in the center as possible. Match it with the center mark on the soaked handle strip and clip the two together. See *Diagram 4*. Cable clips are especially helpful here as the round reed is too heavy for clothespins. Clip one strip on one side of the hoop and one strip on the opposite side. Allow to dry thoroughly (overnight).

Weaving The Base

From the 1″ flat reed, cut seven pieces 43″ long. From the 1″ flat reed, cut eleven pieces 37″ long. From the ½″ flat reed, cut six pieces 25″ long.

Mark the centers (half the length) on the wrong sides. Soak all the pieces for two or three minutes or until flexible. Place the seven longest strips, wrong side up, on a flat surface horizontally, leaving ½″ space between them. Next, lay the six ½″ strips, wrong side up, in the spaces between the long ones. Align the center marks. See *Diagram 5*.

Weave the eleven 37″ strips over and under, beginning with the one in the center and aligning the center marks. At this point, treat the short filler strips as one with the long strip between them. See *Diagram 6* for weaving pattern. Once the base is completed and

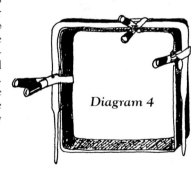

Diagram 4

Diagram 2

Diagram 3

Diagram 3 A

Diagram 5

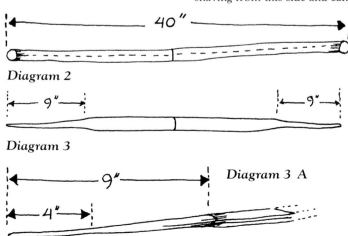

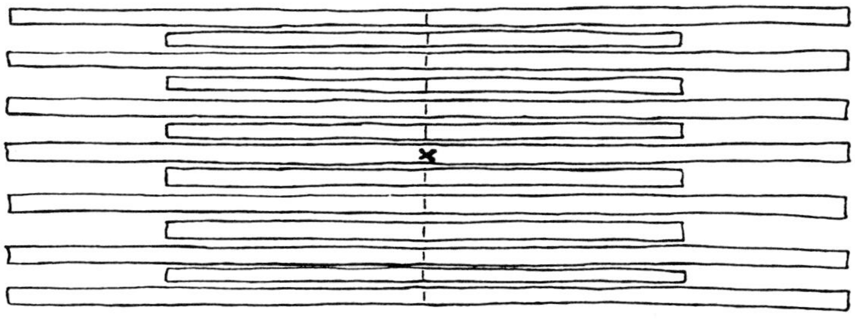

CHEROKEE PICNIC BASKET

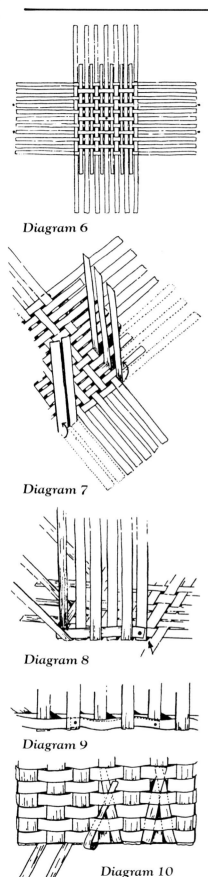

Diagram 6

Diagram 7

Diagram 8

Diagram 9

Diagram 10

trued (measured to be sure the opposite sides are even), mark all the corners so you will know if any slipping occurs. See **Diagram 6**.

Upsett all the longer stakes by bending them, at the base line, all the way over upon themselves (toward the woven bottom) forming a permanent crease. They will stand only temporarily but will all stay upright after the first two rows of weaving have been completed. See **Diagram 7**. Leave the filler strips lying flat.

Weaving The Sides

Begin a long, soaked piece of ⅝″ flat weaver by placing the end on the outside of one of the stakes that originates from underneath the woven bottom. By doing this, the stakes that stand upright first are the ones anchored by a row of weaving on the bottom. See **Diagram 8**. Weave all the way around, wrong side of the weaver against the stakes, in a simple over-under pattern. Upon reaching the beginning stake, continue weaving for three more stakes, ending behind the fourth one, thus hiding both ends behind a stake or a weaver. See **Diagram 9**.

Continue to weave, one row at a time, starting each row in a different spot so as to avoid a buildup of overlapping starting points. Anytime after the fourth row of weaving, tuck the filler strips under the weaving for as many rows as you like. Cut them, as in **Diagram 10**, so the ends are hidden. Weave the sides for ten rows. Although the basic shape is rectangular, allow the corners to "round."

Inserting Loops And Applying Rim

Locate the loops you have formed earlier. Make a mark 2½″ from each end of the "U." Make a mark ¾″ above each of the first two marks. You must scoop out the area between the marks with a sharp knife, cutting away about half the thickness of the reed. See **Diagram 11**. Taper from the notch to the ends until the last inch is about the thickness of flat reed.

For stability and decoration, a strip of ⅝″ flat or flat-oval reed is applied over the last row of ⅝″ weaving. If you are using a prepared

swing handle, you must insert the loop through it before pushing the loops into place. See **Diagram 12**. If you are making your own handle, it can be attached later.

Insert the loops over the fourth stake from each end of the basket on both sides. The ends of the loops should be hidden behind the lower rows of weaving and the notch in the loop should align with the top row of weaving. Apply the soaked piece of ⅝″ rim, holding it in place with clothespins. Overlap the ends and shave some from both ends to lessen the thickness if you are using flat-oval. Begin a soaked piece of 3/16″ flat reed and lash the rim in place by following the usual rim directions. See **Diagram 13**. The rim should resemble **Diagram 14** when it is completed.

Weaving The Top Of The Basket

It is at this point that the stakes lean inward. Bend every stake above the rim toward the inside of the basket, causing them to lean slightly inward. Resume weaving, this time with ¼″ flat reed (soaked). Naturally, as the stakes lean inward, there will be less room between them, particularly at the corners. Taper any of the stakes that come within ⅜″ of another. See **Diagram 15**. Weave, as before, one row at a time for 14 rows, gently pressing on the stakes to make them lean in. Begin pinching the corners so that the basket top will again become rectangular instead of rounding at the corners. For the last five or six rows, make a concerted effort to make the stakes stand straight up again, not slanted. This will help the lid fit comfortably.

Applying The Rim And Lashing

Point all the ends of the outside stakes as in **Diagram 16**, and bend them to the inside. Push them under at least two weavers. Cut the inside stakes flush with the top row of weaving.

Soak two pieces of ½″ flat-oval reed that are long enough to wrap around the rim of the basket and overlap about 2″. Fit the ½″ flat-oval reed around the top, covering

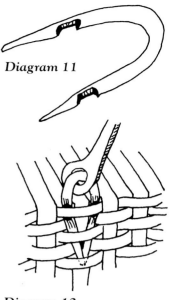

Diagram 11

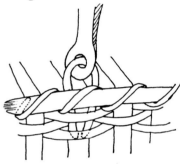

Diagram 12

Diagram 13

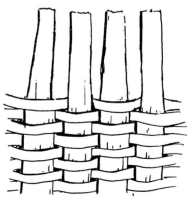

Diagram 14

Diagram 15

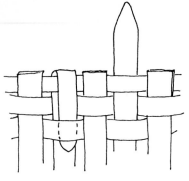

Diagram 16

Diagram 17

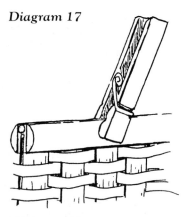

Diagram 18

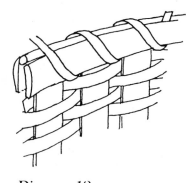

Diagram 19

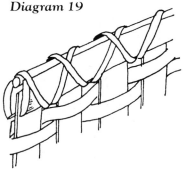

Diagram 20

the last two rows of weaving. Bevel the ends as in **Diagram 17** so there is no bulky overlap. Hold with clothespins. Repeat the same procedure with a strip of ½" flat-oval on the inside. Hold with the same clothespins. Then put a piece of #6 round reed on top and between the two pieces of flat oval, again using the same clothespins. See **Diagram 18**. Lash all three pieces together with a soaked piece of 3/16" flat reed by inserting one end between the two rim pieces, as in **Diagram 19**. Cut the lashing flush with the top of the rim when finished; end the same way you began. Lash in the opposite direction if you wish to have an "X" pattern. See **Diagram 20**.

Making The Lid

Cut six pieces of 1" flat reed 21" long. Cut nine pieces of 1" flat reed 18" long.

Begin, as you did the base of the basket, with the longer stakes and weave the shorter ones over and under, aligning center marks. The woven area should be about 1½" smaller than the opening of the top of the basket on all sides. See **Diagram 21**.

NOTE: Although the directions do not call for filler strips, they may be added, if you wish.

Split all the corner stakes as in **Diagram 22**. Then, with a ¼" or 3/16" soaked weaver, begin weaving around the woven mat, still on a flat surface, and spreading the corner stakes as in **Diagram 23**. Weave one row at a time, starting and stopping as before. Weave as many rows as you need for the lid to fit the basket top. Keep fitting the lid to the top of the basket until it fits and the woven area is just a

"tad" larger than the basket opening. When it fits, upsett the stakes and continue weaving until the lid is 1½" to 2" deep. See **Diagram 24**. Finish the lid with a rim, just as you finished the basket. Pinch the corners of the lid, if needed, to make it conform to the shape of the basket top.

Finishing And Attaching The Handles

Remove the completely dry handles from the form to which they are clipped. With a sharp knife, shaper, and sandpaper (use sandpaper last), remove some of the reed in the rounded corner area. See **Diagram 25**. Next, make two holes in the flat part of the handle with a ¼" drill bit. The first hole must be 7½" from the end of each handle and the second hole must be 8½" from the end of each handle.

Soak the ends of the handle again (at least 30 minutes). Do not soak the whole handle as soaking might cause the top of the handle to lose its shape.

When the ends are flexible, bend them around, going through the previously inserted loops in the basket, and thread the ends through the first hole, from the inside out, and then back through the second hole ending on the inside. See **Diagram 25**. Sand the end smooth with the handle. Allow the loop to dry, holding it in place with a clothespin if necessary. The threading of the handle can be done around the loop after it has been inserted or can be attached just as the swing handle was, before the loop was inserted. **Diagram 26** shows the threaded handle in place.

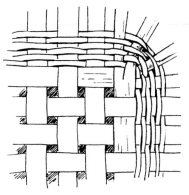

Diagram 23

Diagram 24

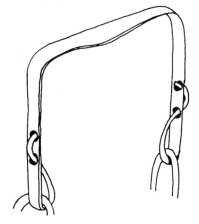

Diagram 25

Diagram 21   *Diagram 22*

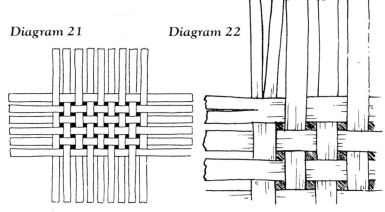

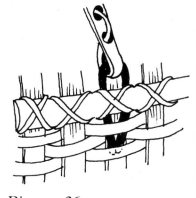

Diagram 26

FISHING CREEL

The prototype for the fishing creel belonged to Carolyn Kemp's grandfather who filled it with trout on more than a few occasions. The only sign of wear can be found on the shoulder strap. It was obviously well made and well cared for over the years.

Materials

#10 round reed
#5 round reed
#4 round reed
Small amount of 3/16" flat or flat oval reed
4' of cloth belting material or a 1'-wide strip of leather

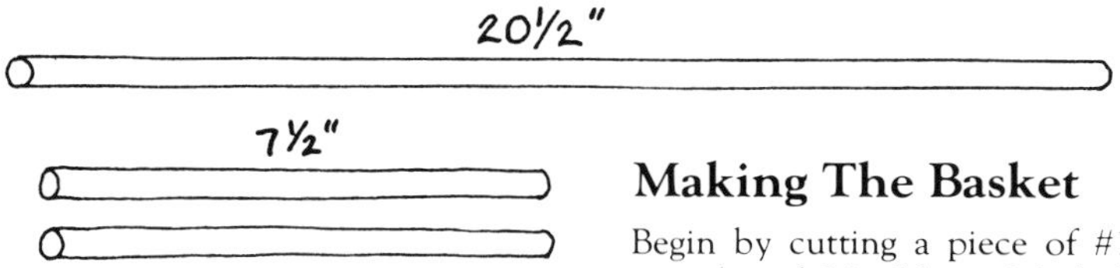

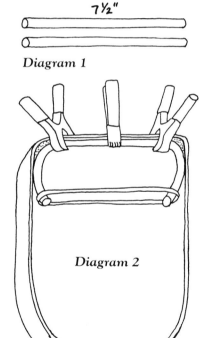

20½"

7½"

Diagram 1

Diagram 2

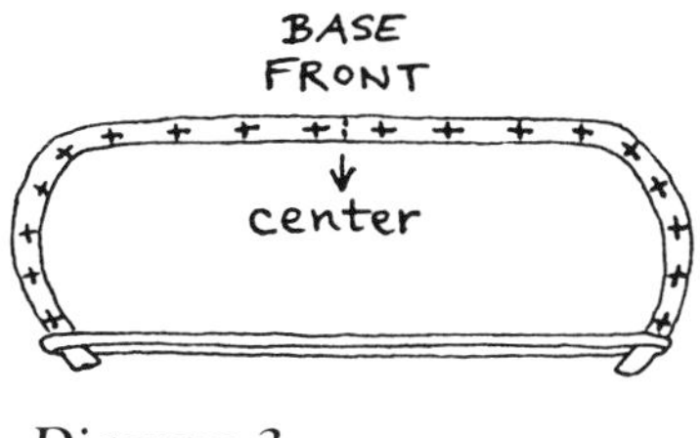

BASE
FRONT

↓
center

Diagram 3

Made with good quality reed, a creel should serve one adequately for a lifetime of fishing. I have been told that rubbing the finished basket with oils helps prolong its life, but have found no documented proof since so little has been written about the making of the creel.

Making The Basket

Begin by cutting a piece of #10 round reed 20½" long. Mark the center at 10¼". See **Diagram 1**. It should be pre-formed to the shape of the basket before you begin. You may find something that works better, but we found a 10" D handle was the perfect mold. As in **Diagram 2**, place the well-soaked #10 reed inside the handle, using cable clips to hold it in place. Tie the ends or use a very heavy rubber band to pull them into shape. Also, cut two pieces of the #10 reed, 7½" long, to be used as the back corner posts.

When the frame is dry and pre-formed, cut 16 pieces, 36" long and 20 pieces, 16" long from the #5 round reed. From the center mark on the formed frame, make marks at 1" intervals. You should have eight marks across the front and five on each end. See **Diagram 3**.

With a sharp knife, split the #10 reed frame in half (lengthwise) so you can push the #5 spokes through. Cut all the way around, leaving approximately 1½" on each end unsplit.

NOTE: Keep the rubber band on the ends of the frame while you weave so it doesn't lose its shape.

Push the 36" spokes through the split frame at the marked spots (from front to back) in pairs, leaving 12" on the front and 24" on the back, which will become the base and the back of the basket. See **Diagram 4**. Use clothespins to hold the spokes in place. Do not put the side spokes in yet.

With a soaked piece of 3/16" flat reed, lash the spokes in place by beginning at one end and wrapping around itself to hold it in place. See **Diagram 5**. Continue lashing across the front. Cut any remaining weaver and end the lashing by tucking it in between the two split pieces. See **Diagram 6**.

Soak a long piece of #4 round reed and begin weaving across the "back to front" spokes in a simple wicker weave as in **Diagram 7**, turning around the last spokes as in **Diagram 8**, reversing directions. Begin making an extra turn around the rim at the corners and insert the 16" spokes on the ends at the marked spots. **Diagrams 9** and **10** show one spoke (on each end) inserted with the extra turn made around the rim.

Any time a weaver runs out, splice on a new one as in **Detail A**.

Continue weaving back and forth across the base, inserting new stakes at the marks and wrapping an extra turn around the rim between rows.

Because of the fullness on the ends of the base, a few extra turns are necessary to "fill in." Simply turn around the spokes marked on **Diagram 11**, reversing directions for a short row.

End the weaving on the base at B in **Diagram 11**. Add another piece into the weaving and with the two pieces, twine across the back, as in

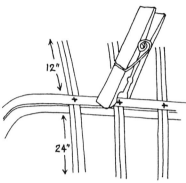

12"

24"

Diagram 4

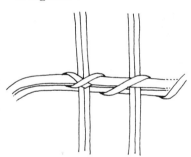

Diagram 5

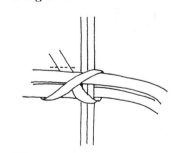

Diagram 6

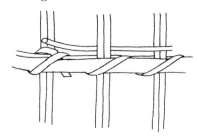

Diagram 7

Diagram 11. Tuck the ends into the weaving.

NOTE: Do some shaping by pushing the weaving toward the front (in the center back). The back should be slightly curved as in the diagram.

Use a very small nail or tack to secure the two 7½″ posts to the ends of the existing frame. Be sure you realize that they are standing up while the frame is flat and has been woven for the base.

Turn the base over so you are now working from the outside of the basket. Begin a three-rod wale by starting three separate weavers, each behind three consecutive spokes and bring each weaver, farthest one to the left first, over the two stakes to the right, behind the next and out to the front. See **Diagram 12**. Begin at post B. Rewet the spokes at this point. Work the three-rod wale all the way around the base, back to A. As you round post C, start to "roll" the spokes upward, fol-

lowing the shaping you did while twining. Continue to B. Using post D or point B as your starting point, work two more rows of three-rod wale all the way around the basket, upsetting the spokes as you weave.

NOTE: If any spoke breaks, replace it by pushing a new one into the weaving.

When you round post D the third time, end two of the weavers by pushing the ends into the weaving. Continue weaving a plain wicker weave (over 1, under 1) all the way up the basket for about 5″.

NOTE: You must control the shape of this basket by your weaving tension and by doing some molding with your other hand, i.e., push in on the back as you weave while you loosen up on the sides and front. After about 3″ of weaving, you must bring all the spokes in very gradually — the front and two sides lean inward, while the back remains fairly straight. See **Diagram 13**. At 5″, the front is as high as it will be.

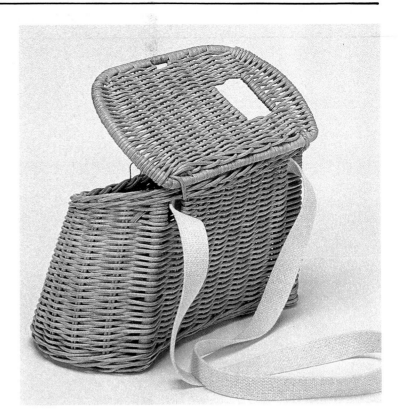

FISHING CREEL

112

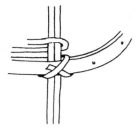

Diagram 8

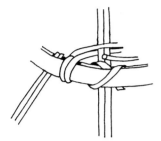

Diagram 9

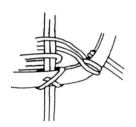

Diagram 10

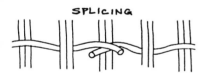

Detail A

Weaving one side at a time, refer to **Diagram 14** and increase the height on the two sides by turning and reversing to post C two times, making an extra wrap around post C. Start a new weaver on the other side and increase to D.

Now turn your attention to the back. Tuck a new weaver in behind the first pair of spokes as in **Diagram 15**. Weave back and forth, reversing directions at the 1st and 8th pair of spokes for eight rows. This creates an opening for the straps. End weavers.

Now, starting three weavers on the back, work one row of three-rod wale all the way around the basket. End the three rods by cutting them on the inside of the basket.

Of each pair of spokes still standing, cut one off flush with the top row. Looking at **Diagrams 16, 17** and **18**, do a closed border by the following means: (1) Bring each spoke behind the one to its right, to the outside, (2) Take them all back to the inside going over the next two and (3) Bring all of them back to the outside going behind the next (4th) spoke. Cut smoothly on the outside.

Making The Lid

Using strong clothespins or cable clips, secure a piece of #10 round reed to the top of the basket, allowing it to lie on the rim. Let the ends overlap 1″-2″. Leave it to dry so the lid will be formed to the shape of the basket. It should be about 29″ long.

Scarf the ends so they lie smoothly and are the same thickness as the rest of the #10 reed when overlapped. You may need to cut a "wedge" from the reed to make the sharp corners on the back. See **Diagram 19**.

Cut the rim in half, lengthwise, from * to * on the front and across the back, leaving about an inch on each end unsplit. NOTE: You need not try to split the back where the two ends overlap; just thin the end on that spoke so it will lie in the scarfed area.

Looking at **Diagram 19**, mark the places for the spokes to be placed, eight spots that are about 1″ apart.

From the #5 round reed, cut seven pieces, 6″ long; seven pieces, 12″ long; and three pieces, 9″ long. There are no side (or end) pieces, only "front to back" spokes. There are two openings in the lid — a small one in the center front and a larger "fish hole" to the left of the center.

Looking at **Diagram 19** and **Detail B**, shave only one end of all the 12″ spokes and two of the three 9″ spokes for about ½″, making them little more than "paper thin" for the last ¼″. Shave both ends of all the 6″ spokes in the same manner. Spoke "I" is the only one that need not be tapered at all. See **Detail B** for shaving ends.

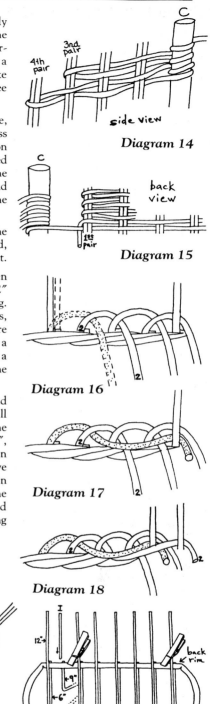

Diagram 14

Diagram 15

Diagram 16

Diagram 17

Diagram 18

Diagram 19

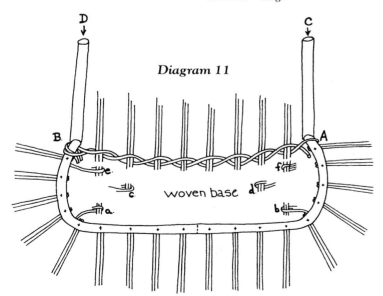

Diagram 11

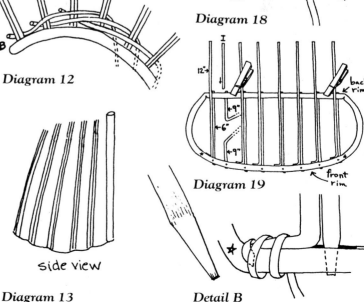

Diagram 12

Diagram 13

side view

Detail B

Soak a long piece of 3/16″ flat reed for wrapping the rim and begin on the left at the * as in the Detail. Wrap solidly. When you reach the spot marked for the first spokes to be inserted, lay the tapered end, bent to the left, of a 12″ spoke on the rim and wrap over it. Immediately, push one end of a 6″ spoke through the rim, flush against the long one, and continue wrapping. See **Detail B**. The next marked spot requires only a single 9″ spoke pushed through the rim. Each pair of the remaining spokes should be treated as the first two, i.e., the long one bent with the wrapping over it and the short one pushed through the rim. End the wrapping as you did on the base.

Insert the other end of the 6″ spokes through the back rim, and insert the other shaved 9″ spoke opposite the first one.

Spoke "I", beside the single at the back, will be inserted later into the weaving when it is done, beside the existing spoke. Cut the ends of the inserted spokes flush with the rim. Try to ignore the long ends of the 9″ spokes (singles) while you are weaving; they will be woven into the lid as you come to them. Wrap solidly, the whole back rim, with another soaked 3/16″ flat reed as

in **Diagram 20**. Begin weaving the lid with a soaked #4 round reed (weaver), referring to **Diagram 20**.

Start on the inside (left) and turn around point "a", the fourth spoke from the left, and end where you began. The ends can be left longer and tucked into the weaving later. Start next on the right side, turn around "b", the fourth spoke from the right and return. Keep on weaving now across the whole top, to point "d" or "e" (depending on the direction from which you approach it). Bend the end of the single spoke "c" to the right and weave it into the lid, joining another weaver wherever it happens to end. At points "d" and "e", the weaving reverses, leaving a "fish hole." Make an extra turn around the first and third spokes throughout this whole area up to points "f" and "g." Spoke "h" weaves into the lid as did "c." When you have woven to within ¼″ of the back rim, end the weaver on the right side.

Make a closed border by the following means: (1) Insert spoke "i" into the weaving beside "h." (2) Beginning with the far left long spoke, bend it, and each subsequent one, to the right, going under 1, over 2 and ending behind

the fourth spoke. Continue with each remaining spoke. See **Diagram 21**. Clip the ends on the inside so they lie smoothly.

Attach the lid to the basket by pushing a piece of soaked reed through the weaving around the back rim of the lid and through the weaving around the back rim of the basket. The spots for attachment are designated by an asterisk (*) in **Diagram 21**. Twist or tie the reed so it won't pull out. The ends can be worked into the weaving to make it more secure.

Push a piece of small round reed or wire into the basket (center) so it will extend up through the center hole in the lid. See **Diagram 22**.

Making The Latch

From the #10 round reed, cut a piece 2¾″ long. Looking at **Diagram 23**, taper one end on one side, for about 1″ to approximately half its thickness at the end. Then on the opposite side from the taper, hollow out an opening, as in the diagram, about 1½″ long. A good way to start the opening is to use a small drill bit, just to get the hole started. From there you should be able to hollow it out with your knife. If the end splits off, use a tiny nail and some "quick glue" to hold the two pieces together at the end.

Attach it to the lid by running a small piece of round reed (or wire) through the opening in the latch and through the lid (hiding the ends in the weaving), making sure the latch will reach through the "holder" you put in the basket that sticks up through the hole in the lid. Another piece of round reed wraps over the latch and down into the lid just to hold the latch in place better. See **Diagram 24**.

Attach the strap by taking it through the two holes on the back and joining the ends on the inside as in **Diagram 25**.

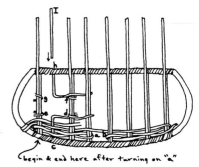

Diagram 20

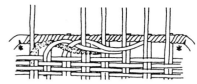

Diagram 21

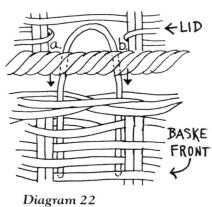

Diagram 22

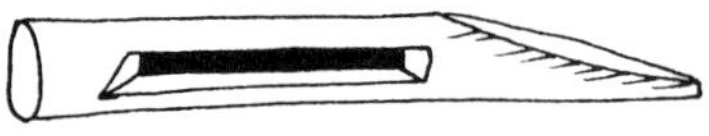

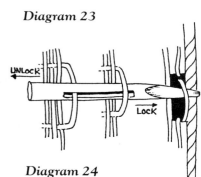

Diagram 23

Diagram 24

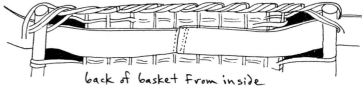

back of basket from inside

Diagram 25

UTENSIL BASKET

UTENSIL BASKET

This is a plaited basket. The base is a plain twill weave but the sides are plaited diagonally or obliquely. The photograph also shows a much larger version that served as my inspiration. The same technique is used in the large one with the only real difference being the decreased diameter at the neck.

Finished Size

5″ x 5″ x 8″, approximate

Materials

½″ flat reed (weavers, stakes, and rim)
#1 round reed (twining around base)
#5 round reed (rim filler)
11/64″ flat reed or ⅛″ strip cut from the ½″ flat (lashing)

Cutting The Stakes And Weaving The Base

To weave base, cut 20 pieces 34″ long from ½″ flat reed. Dye four strips in the color of your choice; rinse and wipe them well to avoid bleeding. Mark the centers of the four colored pieces on the wrong side. Lay two of them horizontally on a flat surface with four natural pieces on each side of them, and align the ends. See **Diagram 1**.

Following the Pattern Chart, weave in the vertical stakes, beginning with the two other colored ones (one on each side of the horizontal center mark).

Diagram 2 shows the base loosely woven only for clarity; the woven base should look more like *Diagram 3*. Measure and true the base to a 6″ square. Soak the #1 round reed and twine all the way around the base, discreetly tucking the ends into the twining itself. See *Diagram 3*.

Forming The Corners And Weaving The Sides

Make a mental note of the location of 1 on **Diagram 3**, as that point will become a corner. As in **Diagram 4**, lift the base and press on the two sides, forcing a corner to form at 1. The colored stakes will have a natural tendency to cross, but you may need to help them along. All the stakes on one side lean now, obliquely; weave them into the other side in an over 2-under 2 twill pattern. See **Diagram 5**.

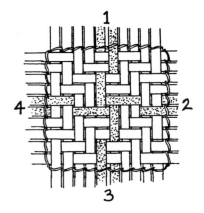

Diagram 3

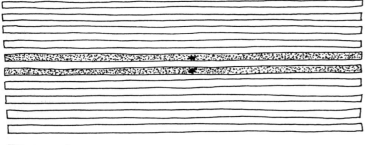

Diagram 1

Pattern Chart

(U = Under, O = Over)

To the right of the center mark (reading from bottom to top):

Row 1, Color: U2, O3, U3, O2
Row 2, Natural: O1, U2, O2, U2, O2, U1
Row 3, Natural: O2, U2, O1, U1, O2, U2
Row 4, Natural: U1, O2, U2, O2, U2, O1
Row 5, Natural: U2, O2, U1, O1, U2, O2

To the left of the center mark:

Row 1, Color: O2, U3, O3, U2
Row 2, Natural: U1, O2, U2, O2, U2, O1
Row 3, Natural: U2, O2, U1, O1, U2, O2
Row 4, Natural: O1, U2, O2, U2, O2, U1
Row 5, Natural: O2, U2, O1, U1, O2, U2

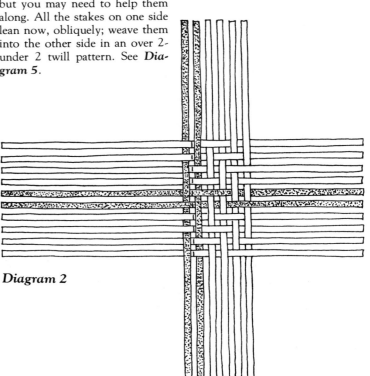

Diagram 2

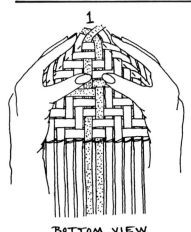

BOTTOM VIEW

Diagram 4

NOTE: *Diagram 4* is drawn looking down at the woven base and *Diagram 5* is a side view once the sides are begun. *Diagram 6* is seen from the same angle as *Diagram 5*. Only three of the stakes have been woven (loosely) in *Diagram 5* whereas all of them (at corner 1) have been closely woven in *Diagram 6*.

Repeat the folding and weaving process at the other three corners. In *Diagram 7*, corners 1 and 4 have been formed and woven.

Once all four corners are formed, continue to diagonally weave all the stakes; they will "fall" into place. To create a stopping place, draw an imaginary line (draw it in pencil if it will help) across the line created when the two colored strips intersect at the top. See *Diagram 8*. Cut the tops of all the stakes at the line. See *Diagram 9*.

Finishing The Basket

Soak a piece of ½″ flat reed that is long enough to reach around the basket twice for an inside and outside rim. Also soak a piece of lashing material. Place the two rim pieces around the top of the basket, allowing 1″ overlap as in *Diagram 10*, with the #5 round between. Hold all the pieces with clothespins and begin lashing as in *Diagram 10* just past the splices. The lasher goes into every fourth space. See *Diagram 11*. See *Diagram 12* for the actual technique, being very sure to note the wrap under the lasher before going to the next space. You may choose to lash into every other space, every third, or every fourth space, but you will probably find the need to lash into the two consecutive spaces where the overlap is located just to secure all the ends of the rim.

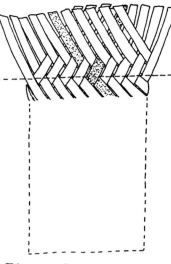

Diagram 8

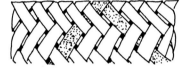

Diagram 9

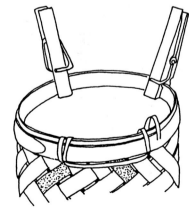

Diagram 10

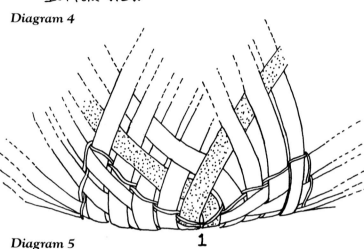

Diagram 5

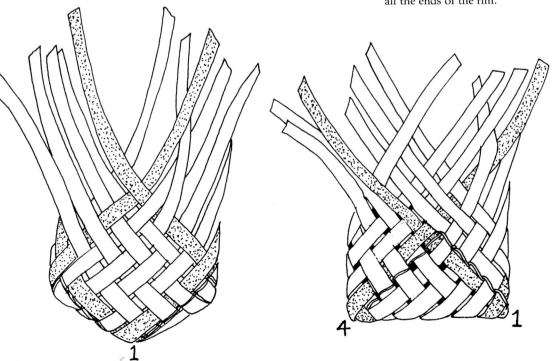

Diagram 6

Diagram 7

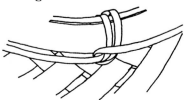

Diagram 11

Diagram 12

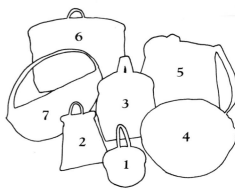

1. NANTUCKET LIGHTSHIP BASKET
   (4″); made by Lyn Siler
2. WEED BASKET; made by Judy
   Wobbleton
3. AMY'S BASKET; made by Lyn Siler
4. TWINED FRUIT BASKET; made by Lyn
   Siler
5. FISHING CREEL; made by Lyn Siler &
   Carolyn Kemp
6. HANNAH'S MARRIAGE BASKET
   (Cherokee Twill); made by Judy
   Wobbleton
7. MELON SLICE (Wall Basket); made by
   Lyn Siler

8. TWILL WEAVE MARKET BASKET;
   made by Louise Grubb
9. OVAL NANTUCKET LIGHTSHIP
   BASKET; made by Lyn Siler
10. SHAKER CAT-HEAD; made by Heidi
    Frazier
11. MELON BASKET; made by Beth Spoon
12. TWILL WEAVE MARKET BASKET;
    made by Carolyn Kemp
13. UTILITY BASKET; made by Carolyn
    Kemp
14. TWINED PLANTER; made by Lyn Siler
15. ORIOLE BASKET; made by Lyn Siler
16. HANNAH'S MARRIAGE BASKET;
    made by Lyn Siler
17. KRISTA'S OVAL (variation); made by
    Lyn Siler

4. VERY SPECIAL BASKETS

... Then there were the "special baskets," for very special people.
Almost always gifts ... as my old friend valued those special
people much more than money.
New babies got one filled with baby things and somehow,
along the way, a tradition began.
Hannah would make her special marriage basket,
and before the wedding, friends and relatives filled in with
other handmade treasures for the bride.

Mine hangs today, after some twenty years, in its place of honor ...
and Hannah wouldn't be pleased that I no longer use it,
but happy, I think, that I cherish it ...
and that it is filled with years of love.

NANTUCKET LIGHTSHIP BASKET

Among the most admired and respected baskets is the Nantucket Lightship Basket. Because it has been made for so many years almost exclusively on the little island of Nantucket, Massachusetts, it has come as something of a surprise to many of us that we, mere "off-islanders," could actually make this lovely basket.

Materials

Mold
Cane (weavers)
Flat oval reed (ribs)
Half round reed (rim)
Ear
Base
¼" Carriage bolt and nut
Brass or copper rivets
Brass escutcheon pins

Diagram 1

Perhaps, because of its isolation on the island, there has been some mystique associated with the Nantucket basket. Like most things, once you know how, it isn't all that difficult. It may require a little more patience than do other baskets, but if you persist, you will be graciously rewarded.

Characteristically, these baskets are made over a wooden mold, have a wooden base, and are woven with cane. The ribs are traditionally made of oak or other hardwoods, but can be made of heavy cane, reed, or any other wood. They usually have an "ear" to which a swing handle is attached, although they are also found with stationary handles and are round or oval.

The instructions here are only one way to make a Nantucket basket. There is basically one way to construct it, but there are many variations of ears and handles. Use these instructions as as guide, but by all means, alter any measurements or techniques that appear to need change. Experiment with different ears, handles, and materials . . . and enjoy!

NOTE: There are wooden molds available from some basketry suppliers. If you do not wish to invest in a wooden mold, there are many containers, particularly plastic, which work well — plastic butter tubs, plastic pails, clay or plastic flower pots. The container must have a ¼" hole in the bottom so the base can be bolted to the container. It should have an indentation in the bottom into which the base will be recessed, but this is not absolutely necessary. It is not hard to find a mold as there is no

one shape it must have — these baskets are made in all shapes and sizes.

The instructions for this basket will be very general because all sizes can be made and will call for cane and reed, not handmade materials. As a general rule, the smaller the mold, the smaller the materials to be used for the ribs. For example, a 3" - 4" basket uses ¼" binders cane, 3/16" or ¼" flat-oval reed; a 5" - 8" basket uses ⅜" flat-oval reed; a 9" or larger basket uses ½" or ⅝" flat-oval reed.

Measuring And Inserting Ribs Into Base

Once you have found a mold and a base to fit, begin by pushing a piece of reed into the groove of the base to determine its depth. With the base on the mold, measure the distance from the base to the bottom of the mold. Add the depth of the groove and use this measurement for the length of all the ribs. See **Diagram 1**.

Begin cutting the ribs, tapering one end 1½" - 2" as in **Diagram 2**. As a general rule, taper the ribs to one half their original width. Insert the ribs into the groove, spacing them about ⅛" apart at the insertion point (closer on very small baskets). If you find your rib material too thick, simply shave a little thickness away with a shaper or knife. You want the rib to fit snugly in the groove of the base, so be careful not to shave away too much. See **Diagram 3** for placing ribs in the base.

NOTE: You must use an uneven number of ribs so that the over-under weave will be continuous.

Diagram 2

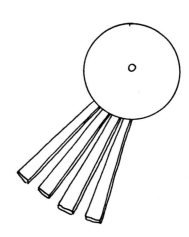

Diagram 3

NANTUCKET LIGHTSHIP BASKET

Diagram 4

When you are sure you have the correct number and spacing of ribs, remove them from the base and soak them in lukewarm water until they are very pliable. When they are well-soaked, reinsert them into the groove. The soaking will have caused some swelling — force them in so when they dry (and constrict) they will still fit. With the carriage bolt, fasten the base (with ribs inserted) onto the mold, using the nut to hold it tight. While the ribs are still wet, bend them all gently and smoothly down around the mold and secure them with one or more heavy rubber bands (this may prove to be a "four-hand" job). On larger baskets, a tire inner tube, cut in 1" -2" strips, works well. Allow the ribs to dry in position. See **Diagram 4**.

Diagram 5

Weaving The Basket

NOTE: The finer the cane, the longer the weaving time (naturally), but the more exquisite the basket. A very large 12" - 14" basket might be woven with 3/16" cane, narrow or medium binders cane, down to fine-fine or superfine cane on the smallest. Some baskets are begun with a very fine cane and changed to a larger size once the weaving starts up the sides.

Taper the end of a 2' (approximately) piece of cane the size you have chosen to use, for about 3" and begin weaving by inserting the end behind a rib or in the groove with a rib. If you find your ribs are loose, allow the first row of weaving to slide into the groove with the ribs making them fit more snugly. Weave over and under the ribs. By using the awl to lift each rib, you must almost "thread" the cane under the ribs. Pull the cane tautly to get a smooth weave. See **Diagram 5**.

Use relatively short pieces of cane (12" - 28") because of the wear and tear each piece gets from the constant "threading" through such a tight space. Be sure the cane is always wet. When one piece runs out, splice a new one by letting the new end hide under a rib. Weave with both pieces until the old runs out on the inside of the basket. Old ends can be trimmed later so they are not noticeable from the inside. See **Diagram 6**.

The rubber band may be removed once the sides of the basket are well established and they will not lose their shape. NOTE: Some people remove the rubber band as soon as they begin to weave; use whichever method works best for you. Take care to pack each row as snugly against the last as possible. Continue adding weavers until the sides reach the height you desire. See **Diagram 7**. Remove basket from mold if you have not already done so.

Diagram 6

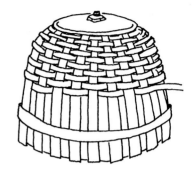

Diagram 7

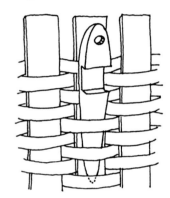

Diagram 8

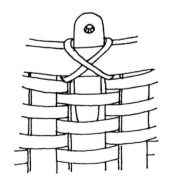

Diagram 9

Diagram 10

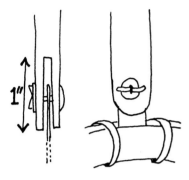

Diagram 11   *Diagram 12*

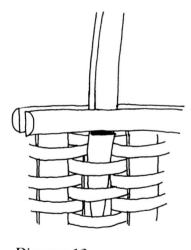

Diagram 13

Finishing Rim, Ear, And Handle

On the last row, taper the weaver for the last 5″ so it is half its width. The weaver should end at the same rib where the weaving began, so the top of the basket will be level.

Before actually applying the rim, select two ribs opposite each other (they will not be exactly opposite because of the odd number of ribs). Mark these two ribs so you can easily find them when you insert the ears.

If you plan to use a notched stationary handle or an ear to which the handle will later be attached, it should be inserted now. If you have a ready-to-use ear, insert it either on the inside or the outside of the basket as in **Diagram 8**, so the notch is placed where the rim will fit into it. You can carve your own ear from any wood of your choice. **Diagram 13** illustrates a stationary, notched handle in place, secured by the rim. If you are using ivory or porcelain knobs, they must be bolted through the handle and rim pieces as in **Diagram 10**.

If you are using brass ears, insert them as in **Diagram 9**. You can make your own brass ears; just cut them with scissors from .010 or .015 gauge brass strips, obtainable from hobby shops or basketry supply shops. **Diagrams 11** and **12** illustrate the handle being attached to the brass ear. A kerf or slit is sawn into the ends of the handles for about ¾″ - 1″. They are then fitted down over the brass ears on both sides and secured with a rivet and washer.

Thoroughly soak (15-30 minutes) a piece of half-round reed that is long enough to reach around the top inside of the basket and overlap itself for about 3″. Use ⅜″ half-round for smaller baskets, ½″ for medium baskets, and ⅝″ for larger baskets.

Bevel one end of the soaked half-round reed to approximately half its original thickness and fit it inside the basket with the top of the rim even with the top of the weaving. Hold the rim in place with clothespins or clamps. Be

sure the rim is level all the way around. When the ends meet, allow them to overlap and mark the beginning of the overlap on both ends with pencil. Remove the rim piece and bevel the second end to fit smoothly over the first. The area of overlap should be no thicker than the rest of the rim. See **Diagram 14**.

Replace rim inside the basket, again clamping, and nail it in four or five places with escutcheon pins, being sure to nail through a rib. Cut the nails off flush with the back of the rib. NOTE: If you are using brass ears, or an un-notched, stationary handle, be sure a nail goes through the rim and the ear of the handle.

Repeat the same procedure and apply the rim to the outside. This time, nail all the way through both rims and a rib, cutting the pins if and when they are too long. See **Diagram 15**. Cut the ribs off flush with top of the rim. See **Diagram 16**.

Next, lay a soaked piece of the wider binder cane on top of the two rim pieces, cane side up, to cover the space between the two rims and the ends of the ribs. With a long, wet piece of smaller cane, begin lashing around the rim. You must force the cane to lie flat as you lash. See **Diagram 17**. Begin and end the lashing either by bringing the end up between the two rim pieces and cutting it flush with the rim or by tucking it behind the weaving on the inside of the basket.

If you have used a notched wooden ear, attach the handle you have chosen by drilling a hole through the ear and the handle and inserting a brass or copper rivet. Secure the rivet with a washer in the recommended manner. If you cannot find a satisfactory rivet, a small bolt and nut will do. Even a wooden dowel can be used or anything that will hold the two pieces together and allow the handle to swing from side to side.

Most Nantucket baskets are painted or sprayed with clear shellac or, more recently, with polyurethane which adds stability and gives the basket a more finished appearance.

Diagram 14

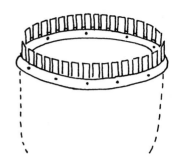

Diagram 15

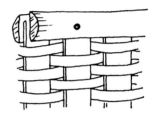

Diagram 16

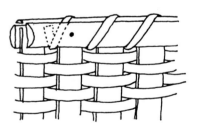

Diagram 17

HANNAH'S MARRIAGE BASKET

HANNAH'S MARRIAGE BASKET

This is one of the most intriguing baskets I have ever seen. Its origin is obscure, although my prototype came from the mountains of North Carolina. I can't imagine there isn't Cherokee influence in the pattern design, if indeed, it wasn't a Cherokee basket.

Finished Size

3″ x 12″ x 9″, approximate

Materials

¼″ flat reed (stakes and weavers)
⅜″ flat-oval reed (rim)
#12 spline or a small strip of white oak (handle)

It is made with white oak, all of which is natural, and well-aged. When I first looked at the basket, a couple of patterns jumped out at me — the "X" and the Diamond. But as I continued to glance at it, especially from a distance, more and more patterns emerged.

The photograph shows the basket made three different ways: All one color as was the original, with colored stakes and natural weavers, and with natural stakes and colored weavers. Each looks very different. Using colored pieces, anywhere, distracts the eye from some of the designs that can be seen in the undyed one, while making others more prominent.

These directions were not easy to write and they probably won't be the easiest you ever followed, but I have never felt a stronger sense of accomplishment than when I finished it and more importantly, understood what I had done. You will feel it too! Many thanks to Judy Wobbleton for helping to "figure it out."

Preparing The Materials

From the ¼″ flat reed, cut 12 pieces 37″ long and 48 pieces 27″ long. Mark the centers on the wrong side of all the stakes. Soak all the pieces for a few minutes.

Lay the 12 longer stakes horizontally on a flat surface, wrong side up.

Weaving The Base

Begin weaving the base with the shorter stakes in the following manner, placing the center mark in the middle of the 12 horizontal stakes.

The following chart reads from **bottom to top** as you look at your base and as you look at *Diagram 1*:

PATTERN CHART

(U = Under, O = Over)

Left Side Of Center	*Right Side Of Center*
Rows 1- 2: U4, O4, U4	Rows 1- 2: O2, U4, O4, U2
Rows 3- 4: U2, O4, U4, O2	Rows 3- 4: O4, U4, O4
Rows 5- 6: O4, U4, O4	Rows 5- 6: U2, O4, U4, O2
Rows 7- 8: O2, U4, O4, U2	Rows 7- 8: U4, O4, U4
Rows 9-10: repeat rows 1-2	Rows 9-10: repeat rows 1-2
Rows 11-12: repeat rows 3-4	Rows 11-12: repeat rows 3-4
Rows 13-14: repeat rows 5-6	Rows 13-14: repeat rows 5-6
Rows 15-16: repeat rows 7-8	Rows 15-16: repeat rows 7-8
Rows 17-18: repeat rows 1-2	Rows 17-18: repeat rows 1-2
Rows 19-20: repeat rows 3-4	Rows 19-20: repeat rows 3-4
Rows 21-22: repeat rows 5-6	Rows 21-22: repeat rows 5-6
Rows 23-24: repeat rows 7-8	Rows 23-24: repeat rows 7-8

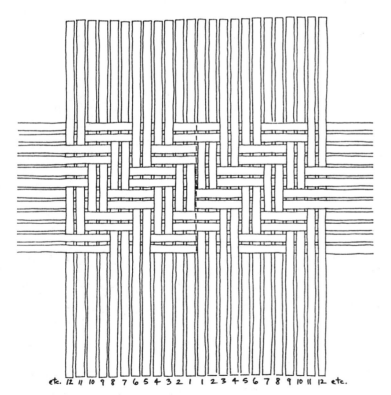

Diagram 1

Pack all the weaving tightly. Measure and true the base to 3″ x 12″. Do not upsett the stakes. Soak a long ¼″ weaver.

Weaving The Sides

As you look at the side nearest you (holding the stakes upright), find the four stakes to the left of the center mark that are coming from underneath the woven base. Begin by weaving around the last three stakes of that group and continue under the next three, over the next three, etc. See *Diagram 2*. Roll the stakes upward as you weave. On this and all subsequent rows, hide the end in the usual manner, overlapping the ends as many stakes you deem necessary to secure and hide them. See *Diagram 3*.

The first six rows are a simple over 3-under 3 twill weave, stepping up one stake each row. Remember to start every row on a different side or at a different spot to avoid a build-up from starting and stopping at the same spot. See *Diagram 4*.

After weaving the six rows of plain twill, check your shape. Make sure you aren't pulling the sides in too much or allowing them to flare too much. You can either pinch the corners to square them or let them "round," as does ours. See *Diagram 5* for six rows of twill, seen as it was begun, from a center mark.

Now the fun begins — Row 7 begins the pattern rows. Following are row-by-row directions for where to start each row:

Row 7: Locate the 9th stake from the left end (either side). Weave over stakes 9, 10, and 11 (O3). From that point, continue U1, O3, U5, O3, U1, O3, U5, etc.

Row 8: At any point there is a U1 (on the last row), begin by weaving over the U1 **plus** the two on each side of it (O5) and continue U3, O1, U3, O5, etc.

Row 9: At any point there is an O5, weave over the center three, under the next three and repeat O3, U3 around.

NOTE: Every third row will be O3, U3, O3, etc.

Row 10: Locate an O3 that is above an O5 on Row 8. Begin O1 with the center one of the O3 and continue, U3, O5, U3, O1, etc.

Row 11: Find a spot you have an O1. Begin under that one **plus**

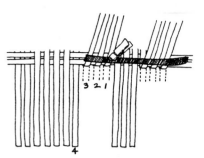

Diagram 2

Diagram 3

Diagram 4

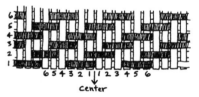

Diagram 5

the two on each side (U5) and continue O3, U1, O3, U5, etc.

Row 12: At a place you have a U5, begin under the center three and continue O3, U3, O3, etc.

Row 13: Find a U3 that is above a U5 (on Row 11). Weave under the center one of the U3 and continue O3, U3, O3, U5, O3, U3, O3, U1, etc.

Row 14: Find the U1. Weave over it and the two on each side (O5); continue U3, O3, U3, O1, U3, O3, U3, O5, etc.

Row 15: Find an O5. Weave over the center three and continue U3, O3, U3, etc.

Row 16: Find an O3 that is directly above an O5. Weave over the center one and continue U3, O3, U3, O5, U3, O3, U3, O1, etc.

Row 17: Find an O1. Weave under that one plus the two on each side (U5). Continue O3, U3, O3, U1, O3, U3, O3, U5, etc.

Row 18: Find an U5. Weave under the center three and continue O3, U3, O3, etc.

From here the pattern repeats itself. In doing it, and writing the directions for it, I found that the simplest process is to make light pencil marks on the row you want to repeat and follow exactly what is done there. Following is a chart of which rows are repeated and their order:

Row 19: repeat Row 17
Row 20: repeat Row 16
Row 21: repeat Row 15
Row 22: repeat Row 14
Row 23: repeat Row 13
Row 24: repeat Row 12
Row 25: repeat Row 11
Row 26: repeat Row 10
Row 27: repeat Row 9
Row 28: repeat Row 8
Row 29: repeat Row 7

After weaving Row 29, begin an O3, U3 starting at a spot there was a U1; go over that one and one on each side (O3). This is not a twill O3, U3, but a regular plain weave. You must begin on this first row of the plain weave to pull the three stakes together so they can be treated as one. See *Diagram 7*.

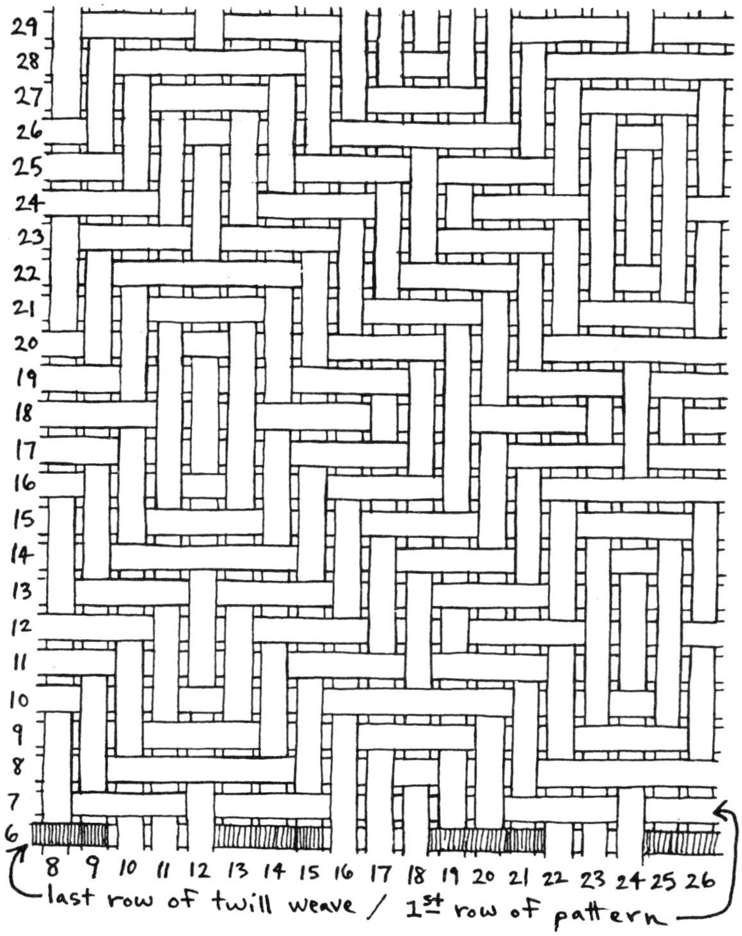

Finishing The Basket

Weave seven rows in plain weave. When they are done, cut two of the three stakes in a group, leaving the outside one. Point it if necessary and tuck it into the weaving inside the basket. See *Diagram 8*.

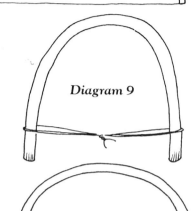

Make the handle by soaking a 16″ piece of spline (if that is what you have chosen to use) until it is pliable. Bend it in the shape you want and tie it as in *Diagram 9* until it dries. Notch it with a knife as in *Diagram 10*, tapering the ends to paper thickness. Insert the handle into the basket, centering it as much as possible as in *Diagram 11*.

Next soak two pieces of ⅜″ flat-oval reed long enough to reach around the basket twice. Scarf or bevel the ends and allow them to overlap about 2″. See *Diagram 12* for applying the rim and holding it in place with a clothespin; see *Diagram 13* for the scarfed ends. Lash the two flat-oval rim pieces on with a ¼″ flat reed, losing the end between the two rim pieces.

Although the directions here reproduce the basket as authentically as possible, the basket would also make a wonderful "tote," simply requiring handles on each side or two swing handles attached by ears or loops.

Diagram 9

Diagram 10

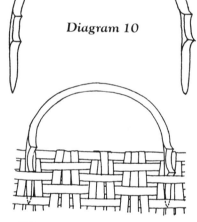

Diagram 11

29 28 27 26 25 24 23 22 21 20 19 18 17 16 15 14 13 12 11 10 9 8 7 6

8 9 10 11 12 13 14 15 16 17 18 19 20 21 22 23 24 25 26

last row of twill weave / 1ˢᵗ row of pattern

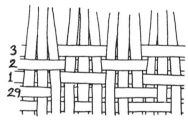

3 2 1 29

Diagram 7

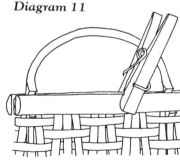

Diagram 12

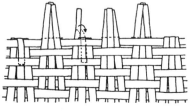

Diagram 8

Diagram 13

FANCY EGG BASKET WITH TWILL TRIM

Many old egg baskets are constructed like this one, i.e., with the bow knot ear and the bottom ribs inserted first, but I have seen only a few that have all the rims covered in the twill weave. Made of white oak with weavers cut about ⅛″ wide, they are truly spectacular. I had to do a lot of experimenting on my own before completing my first one, but was greatly rewarded in the end.

Finished Size

10″ x 10″

Materials

Two 10″ x 1½″ round hoops (frame)
3/16″ or 11/64″ flat reed (weavers)
#6 round reed (ribs)

This basket requires much patience and determination, not because it is so very difficult, but because it is tedious and requires constant concentration. Basic directions are given here for twilling the handle only, but should you choose to cover the rims as well, the directions are as follows: Extend the length of the strips covering the handle to reach to the bottom of the handle and overlap about an inch. You will cut the extra length when the weaving fills in on the bottom so the ends are hidden behind a weaver. Place strips to cover both the rims and push the ends between the two hoops, allowing them to be a little loose as the twill weaving will take up the extra space. The twill weave is worked as you weave around the rims, stepping up or down each row (whichever you prefer). Remember that the twill weaving is going to meet in the center of the hoops and must be in keeping with the pattern when it does so. *Diagram 12* shows the handle and all three rims being twilled.

Making The Handle

Choose one hoop to be the handle. With the splice in the bottom, measure and mark a 14″ area from one side to the other, that will become the exposed handle. The other part of the handle hoop (basket) should be about 17½″.

Measure and mark a halfway point on the rim hoop. Align the two hoops, rim hoop on the inside with its top edge resting on the "exposed handle" mark. Mark all four sides of the intersecting point, but do not tie the hoops together yet. It is easier to work with one hoop while covering the handle. See *Diagram 1*.

Cut as many pieces of flat reed as are required to cover the width of the handle (mine required seven pieces of 11/64″ reed). The strips should end about ½″ past the top of the rim hoop and can be cut to hide behind the ear when it is made. Clothespins will be especially helpful holding these in place.

Start a very long and thin soaked piece of 3/16″ reed behind the handle, leaving the tail free for about ½″. Begin the twill weave around the handle, stepping up one each row. In *Diagram 2*, four rows are done and the fifth is in progress. *Diagram 3* shows the ½″ tail tucked into the weaving on the inside of the handle.

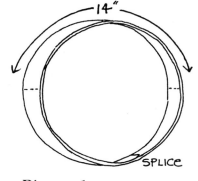

Diagram 1

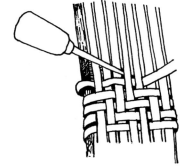

Diagram 2

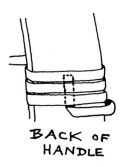

Diagram 3

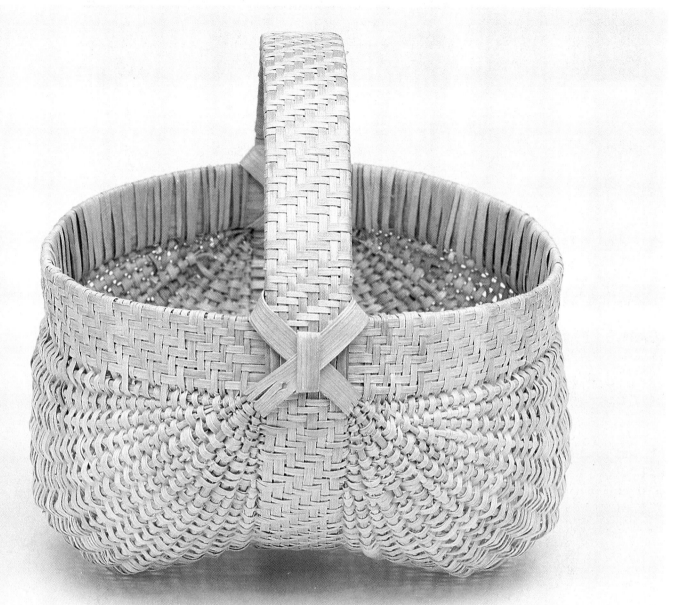

FANCY EGG BASKET

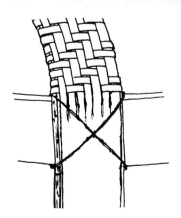

Diagram 4

When the handle is covered, reposition the two hoops and tie them together. If tying isn't secure enough, use a very small nail and nail them together as well. *Diagram 4* shows the two hoops in place with the handle covered.

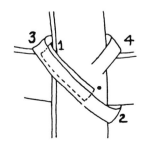

Diagram 5

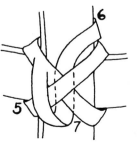

Diagram 6

Making The Ear

Using a piece of soaked ⅜″ flat reed, construct the bow knot ear by the following instructions and *Diagrams 5* through **9**. Starting on the outside at the dot, with the right side out, move to 1, diagonally to 2, up to 3 going over the tail, behind the handle to 4, diagonally on the outside to 5, and diagonally on the inside to 6, making a "twist" on the way. This has put the wrong side out for the moment. Move from 6, down behind the X's in front, emerging from the bottom. Then repeat the

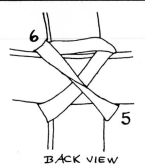

Diagram 7

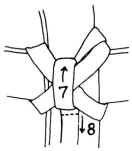

Diagram 8

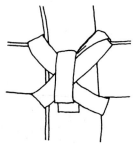

Diagram 9

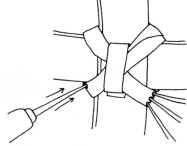

Diagram 10

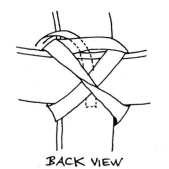

BACK VIEW

Diagram 11

last movement, going behind the X again at 7, ending at 8. Cut the weaver at the dotted line in **Diagram 8**. Notice the right side is out as the "knot" is made. **Diagram 9** shows a finished ear. NOTE: Some of the diagrams do not show the twilled handle, but in reality it has been completed at this point.

Cutting And Inserting The Ribs

The ribs should not be sharpened with a pencil sharpener for this basket, but rather whittled with a sharp knife, as you can get a much longer taper with a knife than with a sharpener. Because you will need to put most of the ribs into the ear at the beginning, they must be almost "pinpoint" sharp, and should begin their taper 1" - 2" from the end.

It is almost impossible to give actual rib measurements for a basket of this kind. There are so many variables that can and do influence the placement and lengths of ribs, such as your weaving tension, the direction in which your ribs lean, etc. I can only give the measurements that have worked for me.

Technically, the first three to five ribs (or whatever number you can get into the ear initially) will be the longest ribs and will form the bottom or "fanny" of the basket. For the first several rows of weaving, make a concerted effort to pull the ribs downward toward the bottom of the basket.

My first three ribs, from the rim down, measured 19", 19", and 18" respectively. These three ribs are inserted into the ear as in **Diagram 10**, with the aid of an awl to split the reed from which the ear is made.

Weaving The Basket And Inserting Secondary Ribs

Begin weaving with a soaked 3/16" flat weaver, by inserting the end under the ear on the inside of the basket or by pushing it between the two hoops as in **Diagram 11**. If you are twilling the rims, the manner in which you begin to weave around the rim is not important (i.e. over 2, or under 2, or

over 1) as long as you follow the twill pattern on the next row. Do whatever your pattern dictates, going over and under each rib and following the twill pattern on the rims.

Diagram 12 shows one row of weaving, with the strips added on the rims for those who have chosen to twill the rims. Otherwise the weaving would resemble **Diagram 14**. When a weaver runs out, splice on a new one as in **Diagram 13**, overlapping the ends enough for them to be hidden behind a rib.

Weave three or four rows before adding any more ribs. **Diagram 14** shows six new ribs added after five rows of weaving. The placement of the additional ribs is optional. Simply remember that the first ones inserted should form the bottom and from there on you will be either adding between the existing ribs to fill in, or adding ribs to form the sides of the basket, or both. From the initial 19" rib, up to the rim, the ribs are gradually going to become shorter and shorter, with the top rib only slightly longer than the distance between ears.

Insert all the ribs you can after four rows of weaving, continue to weave again for four more rows, and add ribs again. Most, if not all, the ribs should be inserted by the 12th row. Use your own judgment concerning the number of ribs needed, keeping in mind that you can't have too many. You might want to change to #5 round reed for the secondary ribs so you can get more in.

Weave some on one side, then some on the other. Never weave all of one side before the other, as the basket will be unbalanced. If you have not twilled the rims, you may stop weaving on the sides after approximately 4" and begin a new weaver in the center at one end. Inevitably, you will have an area to be filled in. Consult Helpful Hints for the three methods of filling in and choose the one that best suits your needs. If you twilled the rims as well as the handle, you will not be able to weave the area in the center, therefore eliminating the "filling in on each side" method; you must choose one of the other methods. See **Diagram 15** for one method.

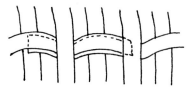

Diagram 12

Diagram 13

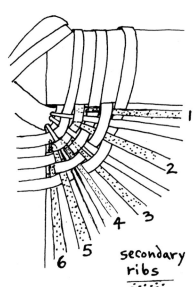

secondary ribs

Diagram 14

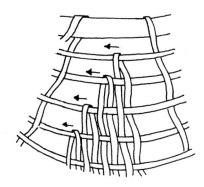

Diagram 15

130

Shaker "Cat-Head" Basket

This lovely basket seems to have originated with the Shakers. It is called a Cat-Head because, when turned upside down, its shape bears a striking resemblance to that of a cat's head.

Finished Size

9″ x 12″, approximate

Materials

½″ flat reed (stakes)
¼″ flat-oval reed (weavers)
16″ #11 or ¼″ spline
  (side handles)
#10 round reed (swing handle)
½″ flat-oval reed (rim)
#5 round reed (rim trim)
3/16″ flat reed or fine cane
  (lashing)

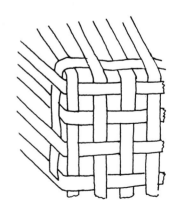

Diagram A

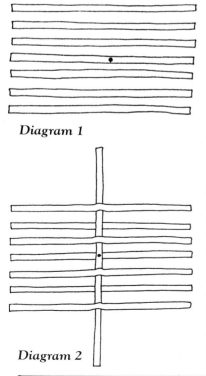

Diagram 1

Diagram 2

The Shakers made their baskets over a mold so the same shape and size could be reproduced every time. Each of yours will vary a little because without a mold you cannot make two exactly alike. Nevertheless, each one will be unique and beautiful in its own right. Patience and concentration are required to form the shape of the Cat-Head, but it can be achieved, even by a beginner, and your efforts will be rewarded with a nice, sturdy, useful basket.

Preparing The Materials

From the #11 spline, cut two pieces 7½″ long. Place the two pieces in cool water to soak for at least 20 minutes. After they are thoroughly soaked, remove them from the water and bend them to form a "U." Secure the "U" shapes by tying a string around them or by using a heavy rubber band. The pieces must dry in this shape for later use. See *Diagram A*.

Cutting The Stakes And Weaving The Bottom

Cut 14 pieces of the ½″ flat reed, 28″ long. Mark the centers of two pieces on the wrong (rougher) side with pencil. Soak all 14 pieces for a minute or two in cool water.

Place seven of the soaked stakes horizontally, on a flat surface, wrong side up, making sure the fourth or middle stake is the one with its center marked. These stakes should be approximately ⅜″ apart, with all ends aligned. See *Diagram 1*.

Once these seven stakes are in place, weave the other marked stake perpendicularly, over and under the other stakes. Be sure to match the two center marks. See *Diagram 2*.

Now weave the other six stakes over and under, three on each side of the middle stake, making sure the weaving is alternating on each row. You have now formed the bottom of the basket. Measure and true the base to a 6″ square. See *Diagram 3*.

Upsetting And Weaving The Sides

Upsett the sides by bending each stake upward and over upon itself. Be sure the "bend" is formed exactly along the line of the perpendicular stake. See *Diagram 4*.

NOTE: The stakes will not remain upright, but making a permanent crease at the base of the stake is important.

The care you should take to shape this basket cannot be stressed too emphatically. Most importantly, the stakes should not be made to stand upright, but rather to lean outward as the weaving is done, especially at the corners.

First, soak one long strip of the ¼″ flat-oval reed (weaver) for a couple of minutes. If your reed is especially thick, as is sometimes the case with flat oval, shave some of the thickness off the top or oval side for about 1½″ with your knife. (This is necessary because the two ends will overlap each other; thinning eliminates some of the bulk.)

Notice, when you look at the woven bottom of the basket, that some of the stakes originate underneath the weaving and some are on top. Begin weaving with a soaked ¼″ weaver by placing the end on the outside of one of the stakes that originates from under the weaving. (Make sure the right or oval side of the weaver is on the outside of the basket.) See *Diagram 5*. The next row of weaving will pick up the other stakes.

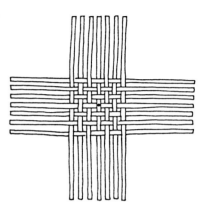

Diagram 3

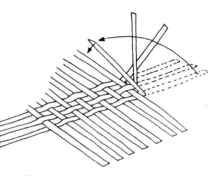

Diagram 4

Diagram 5

SHAKER "CAT-HEAD" BASKET

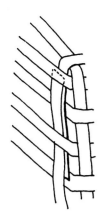

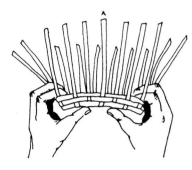

Diagram 6

Diagram 7

Diagram 8

Instead of trying to make the stakes stand upright, push them outward (as is their natural tendency). Do not pinch the corners; make every effort to force the corners to lean outward, even though they will have a tendency to pull in as you weave around them.

When you have woven over and under all the way around the basket, and are back to the starting point, allow the two ends to overlap to the fourth stake. Cut the weaver so the end is hidden behind a stake. The end of a weaver need never show from the inside of the basket. See *Diagram 6*.

NOTE: Check corners after every row to make sure they are leaning outward and becoming nicely rounded. Clipping the two corner stakes together 6″ or 7″ from the bottom also helps round the corners.

Begin weaving the next row, and each new row thereafter, in a different place so as not to get a build-up from constantly starting and stopping in the same place.

When you have woven three rows around, begin the Cat-Head shaping process by pressing upward on the center three stakes and pulling the corners downward simultaneously. This will need to be done after every row of weaving until the bottom is firmly in the correct shape. See *Diagram 7*.

Continue to weave, one row at a time, making the diameter "grow" with every row. When the sides reach a height of 2½″ to 3″, the diameter should reach its fullest point. With a 6″ square base, the diameter should reach approximately 10″ at the fullest point.

Shaping The Top Half Of The Basket

When the sides are as full as you want them, begin to press inward on the stakes as you weave. If pressing on the stakes doesn't bring the sides in enough, give an extra "tug" on the weaver occasionally to bring them in. The top diameter will vary from one basket to the next, but should be approximately 8″ - 9″.

When the height has reached approximately 8″, stop weaving and rewet the tops of the stakes. You will find that half your stakes are behind the last weaver and half are in front. With scissors or wire cutters, cut off the inside stakes even with the last row of weaving. Then point all the outside stakes. Bend the pointed stakes over and insert them into the weaving inside the basket, making sure they reach at least to the third row of weaving, if not further. See *Diagram 8*.

Notching And Inserting The Ears

The two pieces of spline you soaked and shaped will now become your "ears." On each side, measure 2″ from the end and mark with a pencil. Make a second mark ⅝″ above the first one. See *Diagram 9*.

Next, with a sharp knife, make a cut about halfway through the spline on both the marks. Then scoop out half the reed's thickness. Once the notch is made, taper the ends of the reed gradually until the very end is little more than 1/16″ thick. See *Diagram 10*.

Looking at *Diagram 11*, slide the ear through the hole on the swing handle. It may be necessary to whittle or sand a little away from the ear for it to fit comfortably through the hole. With the handles on the ear, slip the ends of the ears into the weaving on the inside of the basket. See *Diagram 12*.

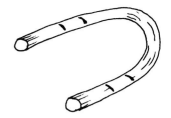

Diagram 9

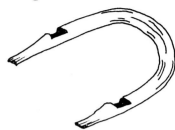

Diagram 10

SWING HANDLE

Diagram 11

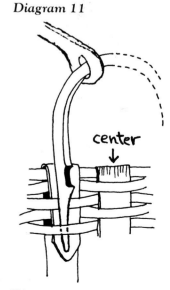

center

Diagram 12

SWING HANDLE

Diagram 13

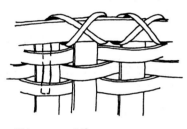

Diagram 14

Diagram 15

Applying The Rim And Lashing

Apply a piece of soaked ½" flat-oval reed around the outside top rim of the basket, holding it in place with clothespins. Allow the ends to overlap about 2", but shave some of the oval off the bottom piece so the two overlapped pieces won't be too bulky.

Next, place another wet piece of ½" flat oval around the inside of the basket, fitting it into the notch in the ears and overlapping the ends as before. Hold both pieces in place with the same clothespins. See *Diagram 13*.

Place a piece of #5 round reed between the two rim pieces, still holding everything in place with the same pins. See *Diagram 14*. NOTE: If you are having trouble fitting the #5 round reed into the ear notch, trim a little thickness off the side of the reed that fits against the spline.

Finally, with a long piece of soaked 3/16" flat-oval reed or medium cane, lash all the rim pieces together following the lashing in *Diagram 14*. Tuck both ends into the weaving where they are the least visible. Use your awl to open up the spaces for the lasher. If you wish, lash in the opposite direction as well, forming an "X" and again hiding the ends behind a weaver. See *Diagram 15*.

The photograph shows a swing handle and a carved handle. If you are interested in carving your own handle, use #14 or #15 round reed. Pre-form it around an 8" or 10" square hoop (whichever fits your basket best), as in *Diagram 16*. Naturally you must soak the large round reed thoroughly before forming it. Mark off the area you want to carve and do so by taking a wedge out of the reed from both sides of the line you made. See *Diagram 17*. Sand well (an emery board works well for the slanted sides) and remove some of the reed on the inside of the corners. See *Diagram 18*.

Make your own notch on either the inside or the outside and taper the ends. See *Diagram 19*.

Experiment with other sizes by using other width reeds for stakes. Remember, you will have to increase or decrease the lengths also. For example, to make a 4" base, use 10 pieces of reed 18" long. The fullest point should be about 7".

Diagram 16

Diagram 17

Diagram 18

Diagram 19

ORIOLE BASKET

The Oriole Basket is so called, obviously, because it looks very much like an oriole's nest. Like all other baskets, it can be useful as well as decorative. It is nice hanging or sitting, and because the frame is usually hand-cut oak, it is sturdy.

Finished Size

7″ x 12″, approximate

Materials

Oriole frame (2-piece set)
¼″ flat reed (weavers)
½″ or ⅜″ flat-oval reed (ribs)
#6 round reed (ribs)

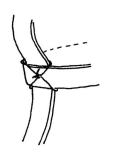

Diagram 1

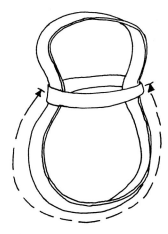

Diagram 2

The original, which I used as a model, had four hand-cut flat oak ribs, two on either side of the frame, and twelve smaller, rounded ribs up the sides. The bottom is fairly flat (or with a slight "fanny") and is the widest part of the basket, which decreases in diameter from bottom to top. The top of the basket is half the diameter of the bottom.

The instructions given here call for ½″ flat-oval reed for making the four flat ribs, which should be practically inflexible. They can be made from several other materials. I suggest using ½″ flat-oval reed only if it is nice and sturdy; if you don't have access to very firm ½″ flat-oval, use three ribs on each side of the frame made of heavy ⅜″ flat-oval reed. It has been my experience that ⅝″ flat-oval reed is too heavy. There are flat, hand or machine cut ribs available from some sources almost identical to flat Melon Basket ribs. I have even made my own from very thin oak veneer which can be cut with scissors. Whatever you use, it is a fun basket to make and own.

Securing The Frame And Measuring The Ribs

Sometimes the two pieces of the Oriole frame come already attached. If not, simply slide the round hoop over the keyhole-shaped part and tie with a waxed string as tightly as possible. If you aren't absolutely sure that the two pieces are securely in place, nail them together with a small, thin nail. See *Diagram 1*.

Once the frame pieces are secured, measure from the intersecting point of the two pieces all the way around to the intersection on the other side. See *Diagram 2*. The measurements should be approximately 21″ on the standard 6″ x 13″ frame. Based on this measurement, cut the four ribs that will be placed in the bottom of the basket by subtracting 1″. In other words, if you measured 22″, then cut the four pieces of flat-oval 21″.

Constructing The God's Eye

NOTE: A three-point lashing may be used as well as a God's Eye.

Select two pliable weavers that are at least 6′ long, for making the God's Eye. Soak them in cool water for 1 or 2 minutes. NOTE: The flat reed has a right and a wrong side. The edges of the right side are slightly beveled; the wrong side is absolutely flat. Begin by placing the wrong side against the hoops. When weaving the basket you need not be concerned with the wrong and right sides.

Referring to *Diagram 3*, begin with the weaver on top of the hoops at the dot. Move up and behind 1, diagonally to 2, behind 2, diagonally to 3, behind 3, diagonally to 4. From 4, move to 1 and repeat the entire counterclockwise procedure five more times. Notice that the starting point (end of reed) is covered as the weaver moves from 2 to 3.

The finished God's Eye will have six revolutions, counting from the back, and will look like *Diagram 6*. The weavers must not overlap each other as any overlap will cause too much bulk. It should lie absolutely flat.

Do not cut the rest of the weaver. Instead, secure it at the rim with a clothespin and make the other ear. It should end on the right rim.

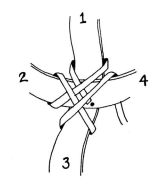

Diagram 3

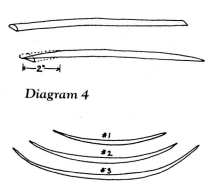

Diagram 4

Diagram 5

Diagram 6

ORIOLE BASKET

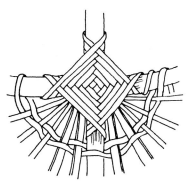

Diagram 7

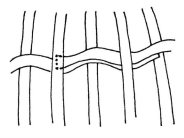

Diagram 8

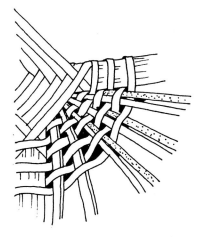

Diagram 9

Making And Inserting The Ribs

Pick up the four pieces of ½″ flat-oval you have already cut. With a sharp knife, taper all the ends so they are approximately ¼″ wide at the ends. The tapered area is about 2″. See **Diagram 4**.

From the #6 round reed, cut two each of the following ribs, one for each side. They are numbered 1-3, counting from the rim downward:

> #1 - 12″
> #2 - 16″
> #3 - 21″

Sharpen the ends of the six round reeds with a pencil sharpener or knife and number them as they are cut. See **Diagram 5**.

Insert all the ribs: #1 under the rim, #2 under #1, and #3 under #2. Then insert the two flat-oval ribs on each side. All the ribs are placed behind the God's Eye, pushed in as far as they will go without protruding through the weaving of the God's Eye. See **Diagram 6**.

NOTE: Try inserting all the ribs at once and then begin to weave. If you have too much trouble keeping the ribs in place as you weave the first two rows, take the round ribs out and weave two or three rows using only the flat oval ribs. Add the other three ribs and continue weaving.

Weaving The Basket

Rewet the remainder of the weaver with which you made the God's Eye, and begin weaving by first making one complete revolution around the rim. This prevents the first row from pressing on the God's Eye too much.

Then begin the first row according to **Diagram 7**. The weaving is shown loosely for clarity only; it should be very tight and fit snugly against the ear.

When you have about 3″ of weaver left, you need to splice on a new one. Referring to **Diagram 8**, lay a new, soaked weaver on top of the old one and weave with both until the old one runs out, continuing with the new one. You never want to splice on a rim, so if you see this about to happen, backtrack a few ribs and add the new weaver.

Preparing And Inserting The Secondary Ribs

After weaving seven or eight rows, cut, sharpen, and insert the following ribs from #6 round reed:

Insert 8″ ribs above and in the same place with #1
Insert 12½″ ribs above and in the same space with #2
Insert 17″ ribs above and in the same space with #3

See **Diagram 9**.

Resume weaving for four more rows. If you think you need more ribs, add them wherever you think they are necessary (the six secondary ribs added here are not usually enough). After adding all the ribs you need, resume weaving. Do not be alarmed when the over-under pattern is interrupted. Continue weaving, going over and under every rib, even if two are occasionally the same. The pattern will correct itself on the second row after adding the new ribs.

Finishing The Basket

Because of the shape of this basket, there will be an area that does not fill in evenly, very much like the full areas of the egg basket. After adding all the ribs needed, begin a new, soaked weaver in the center of the unwoven area. Consulting **Diagram 10**, fold the weaver in half over the rim. Use clothespins frequently to keep the ribs spaced evenly. You are weaving now with one end at a time, one side moving outward to the right and the other moving to the left. Add on new weavers just as you would anywhere else.

The weaving will fill in first on the rim. Squeeze the weavers in until you can no longer fit another one in around the rim. Fill the spaces in by one of the two following methods: (1) Turn around the first rib, reversing just as you did around the rim (See **Diagram 11**) or (2) Cut the weaver on the inside of the basket and begin a new one going in the opposite direction. You may slide the new end over a weaver already in place, or just leave the end sticking out inside the basket. You can go back later and trim the ends inside the basket (See **Diagram 12**).

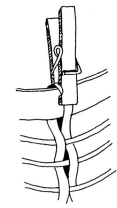

Diagram 10

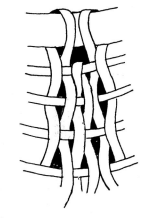

Diagram 11

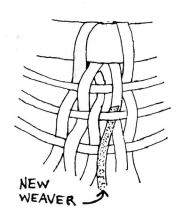

NEW WEAVER ⟵

Diagram 12

SQUARE RIBBED BASKET

This is essentially a square egg basket made by using two square hoops of the same size, instead of round ones. The secret to this basket is pre-forming the ribs so they form the same angle (curve) as do the corners of the hoops.

Finished Size

10″ x 10″ x 10″, approximate

Materials

#6 or #6½″ round reed (ribs)
¼″ flat reed (weavers)
Two 10″ x 10″ square hoops (frame)
3/16″ flat reed or cane (handle braid)

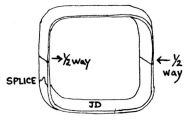

Diagram 1

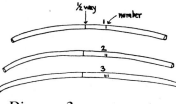

Diagram 2

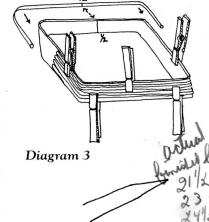

Diagram 3

Diagram 4

Basically, it is constructed like the egg basket, with the ribs inserted in the same order (i.e. 1, 2, 3, 4, 5). A three-point lashing can be used for the ear (as shown here), as well as a four-point lashing or God's Eye. Any size square or rectangular basket may be made like this one, by using the same process of pre-forming the ribs. You can "sight" the rib lengths after they are pre-formed (after the ear is made), by holding them from one side to the other. Simply cut all the ribs longer than they need be, pre-shape them, and trim each end an equal amount until you achieve the desired shape.

If you are a novice, "sighting" may not be for you. But, when you feel ready, attempt your measuring "by eye," so you can become inventive and creative. Use these measurements only as a guide — if you think a rib should be longer, by all means, lengthen it!

Preparing The Materials

Measure the circumference of two 10″ x 10″ hoops, starting at a point as nearly in the center of one side as you can. Divide the circumference in half, making a pencil mark on the side opposite your first mark. See *Diagram 1*. Decide which is to be your handle, and place an initial or some mark in the inside of the bottom.

Measure and cut two each of the following ribs from the #6 round reed, numbering them as you cut:

Primary Ribs	Secondary Ribs
#1 - 17½″	#1s - 18″
#2 - 19″	#2s - 19½″
#3 - 20½″	#3s - 20″
#4 - 20″	#4s - 19″
#5 - 18″	

When all the ribs are cut, pencil mark a halfway point on all the ribs. See *Diagram 2*.

Place all the ribs in a container to soak; use a container large enough so you don't have to bend or curve the ribs while they are soaking. Soak them at least 30 minutes (longer won't hurt), or until they bend easily without cracking. When they are very pliable, align the center marks on the ribs with the center mark on the hoops and bend them, one at a time, around the hoop. Secure them with clothespins in several places so they fit snugly. Several ribs will fit on each side of the hoop and can be held with the same pins. See *Diagram 3*.

NOTE: Although breakage is rare, you might want to soak a couple extra ribs and pre-form them at this time also. If so, cut them 20½″, since that is the longest size rib; they can be shortened to the desired length.

Allow the ribs to dry thoroughly, perhaps in sunlight, for several hours or overnight. When they are completely dry, remove the ribs from the hoops and point all the ends with a pencil sharpener or sharp knife (as sharp as a pencil point). See *Diagram 4*.

Securing The Hoops

Since you have already measured the halfway points on the hoops, all you need do is fit the two hoops together by placing the center mark in the middle of the other hoop. See *Diagram 5*. Notice that the handle hoop is on the outside.

To be sure your hoops are centered, measure one side all the way around from one handle to the other. Then measure the other side, from one handle to the other.

Make adjustments if necessary. (Be sure you haven't put the splice on the handle.) See *Diagram 6*.

When the hoops are in place, and you are sure of their position, make a pencil mark on all four sides at the intersecting points. Tie the hoops securely in place with waxed string; if you feel they aren't secure enough, use a small tack, nailed from the inside out. See *Diagram 7*.

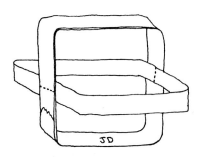

Diagram 5

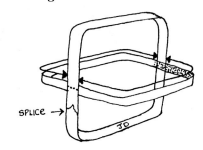

Diagram 6

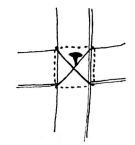

Diagram 7

Wrapping The Handle

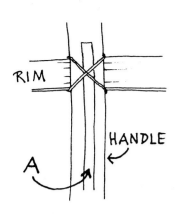

Diagram 8

Cut a piece of 3/16″ flat reed 3″ longer than the handle area measures. (The diagrams will appear upside down, as it is easier to work with the handle toward you.) Slip one end of the 3/16″ flat strip (A) under the string with which you tied the hoops. This strip goes on the outside of the handle. See *Diagram 8*.

Begin a very long (approximately 6′) soaked 3/16″ weaver (B) by slipping the end between the rim and the handle on the inside of the hoops. See *Diagram 9*. Begin wrapping the handle by bringing the weaver B around the handle, over A, four times (more on larger baskets). See *Diagram 10*. At this point, clothespin B in place and insert three pieces of cane that are at least 3½ times as long as the area to be covered (the handle) in the following manner:

1. Mark the center or halfway point on all three pieces of cane on the wrong or flat side.

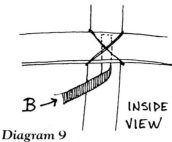

Diagram 9

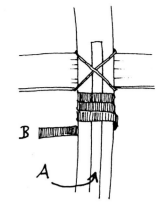

Diagram 10

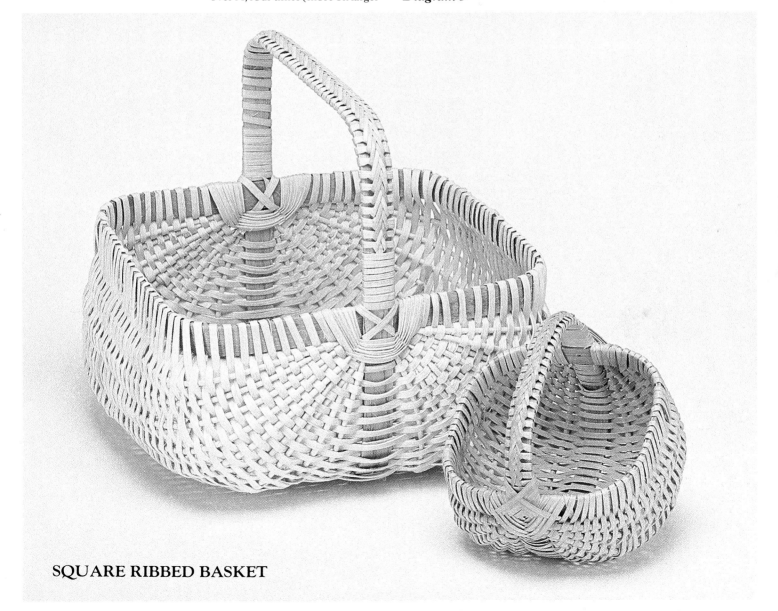

SQUARE RIBBED BASKET

2. Slip one piece (C) under A, placing the center mark directly under A, flat side up.

3. Make one complete revolution around the handle with B, going over A.

4. Slip the second piece (D) under A, again aligning the center mark directly under A, flat side up.

5. Make another revolution with B, as before.

6. Slip the third piece (E) under A, just as you did C and D.

7. Make another revolution with B, as before.

Now, all three pieces are inserted and should look like **Diagram 11**. NOTE: The whole procedure will be easier if you can remember that following every movement with cane, weaver B makes one complete turn around the handle, every time going over A. Use clothespins as needed.

Look at **Diagram 12 A** and begin braiding by bringing the left half of C down, cane side up, over D and E, and under A, entering from the right side and emerging left. Now bring the right half of C down, forming a figure eight and take it

under A and under the first piece of cane (the left half), entering from the left and emerging right.

Next, make one complete turn around the handle, over A, with weaver B. You will find you must give a tug on the cane to tighten it in place and it must remain tightly in place, hence the need for clothespins. See **Diagram 12 B**.

Now repeat the braiding process in the same manner with D, then with E, remembering to make a complete wrap around each with B. NOTE: The right half of the piece of cane may be used first, then the left. The important thing is to be consistent.

Diagram 13 shows strips C and D braided once and strip E in the process. **Diagram 14** illustrates four braids completed.

The next step is to bring strip D down for its braid under A. Naturally, keep repeating the process until there is only about 1″ left for room for four or five final wraps. End the braiding as in **Diagram 15**, bringing all the pieces down in X fashion and covering the ends with solid wrap-

ping. End B on the inside, slipping the reed down between the rim and the handle just as you began. Trim any excess reed.

Constructing The Ear

Select a long (at least 8′) weaver for constructing the ear, coil it small enough to fit in your container, and soak 1-3 minutes. Don't oversoak.

Begin the ear by placing the end of the weaver behind the intersecting points of the hoops, wrong side of the weaver against the hoops, leaving ½″ free. Following the numbers in **Diagram 16**, start at the dot and make an X over the intersecting point. Be sure to take the weaver over the free end when moving from 2-3.

Then, as in **Diagram 17**, begin the actual ear by bringing the weaver over the top of the handle hoop, up and around the right rim (6), down to (7), under the handle hoop and up to the left rim (8). Repeat this procedure, moving from one side to the other, keeping the wrong side of the weaver against the hoops, until you have six rows on both sides. You must count rows from the top of the rim. NOTE: If the loose end of the weaver (at the dot in **Diagram 16**) is in your way after the first revolution, cut it off. Make the ear as tight as possible.

The finished ear should look like **Diagram 18**. Do not cut the weaver. Rather, secure it at the rim with a clothespin.

Inserting Primary Ribs Into Ear

The finished ear has four openings — one underneath each rim (2) and one on each side of the bottom or handle hoop (2). Insert awl into each of these spaces and move it around enough to open the space even more as in **Diagram 19**.

Insert the #1 ribs into the openings just underneath the rim, pushing and twisting at the same time, until

Not flatround?

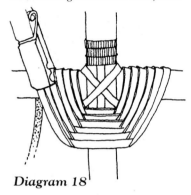

Diagram 18

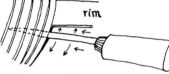

Diagram 19

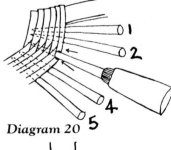

Diagram 20

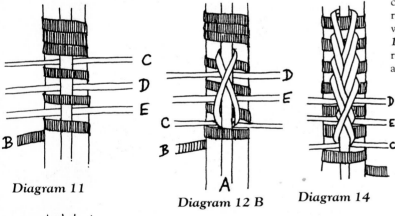

C
D
E
B

Diagram 11

D
E
C
B

Diagram 12 B

D
E
C

Diagram 14

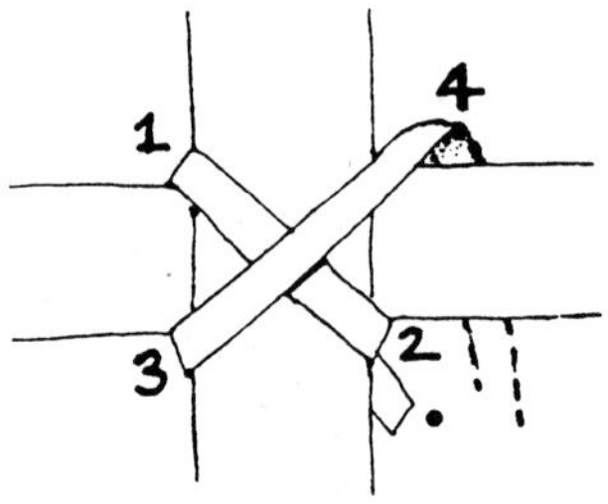

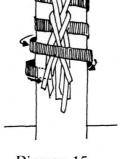

Diagram 16

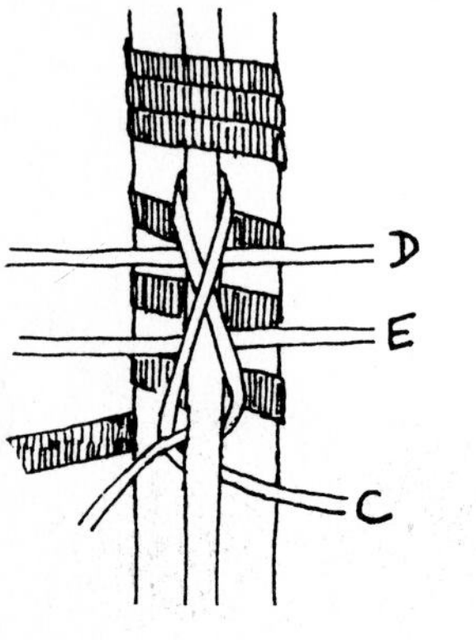

D
E
C

Diagram 12 A

C
D
E

Diagram 13

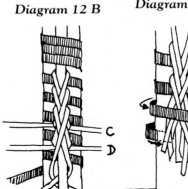

Diagram 15

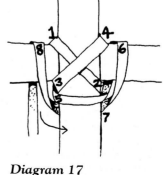

Diagram 17

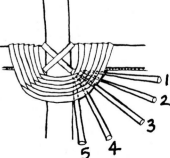

Diagram 21

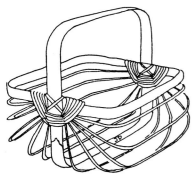

Diagram 22

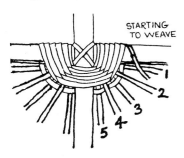

Diagram 23

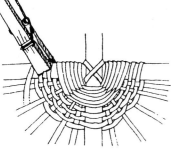

Diagram 24

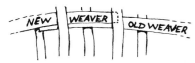

NEW WEAVER | OLD WEAVER

Diagram 25

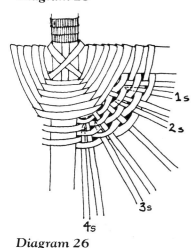

1s

2s

3s

4s

Diagram 26

they feel secure. Insert one on each side of the basket.

Next, insert the #2 ribs into the same space as #1, underneath #1. Insert the #5 ribs into the space on either side of the handle hoop (bottom of basket). Insert the #4 rib in the same space with the #5 rib, above #5.

Referring to **Diagram 20**, make a hole in the reed between the #2 and #4 ribs. This space was formed as a flat area when you were making the ear by keeping the flat side of the weaver down. Move the awl back and forth again to open up this space. The awl actually splits the reed here. Insert the #3 rib in this opening, on both sides. All the ribs are shown inserted (only on one side of the basket) in **Diagram 21**.

With all the primary ribs in place, the basic skeleton of the basket is now formed. If the shape doesn't look right, adjust the ribs now. The basic skeleton should look very much like **Diagram 22**.

Weaving The Basket

With the rest of the weaver you secured at the rim with a clothespin, begin to weave by bringing the weaver behind the rim, over rib #1, under #2, over #3, under #4, over #5, under handle hoop, over #5 (on the other side), etc. See **Diagram 23**. Rewet weaver at any time if dry or stiff.

NOTE: If the ribs "pop out," just put them back in and continue to weave. You must treat them gently, but firmly, making the weavers fit in as close as possible to the ear.

Weave five rows as in **Diagram 24**. If any weaver remains after five rows, leave it hanging free. Now weave five rows on the other side of the basket. After five rows you need to add secondary ribs.

When you have 2" – 3" of any weaver left, you need to splice on a new one. Referring to **Diagram 25**, simply lay the new, wet weaver on top of the old one, hiding the ends if possible. Weave with both the old and the new weavers until the old one runs out, then continue to weave with the new one. You never want to run out on the rim, so if you foresee this might happen, backtrack a few ribs and add the new weaver.

Preparing And Inserting The Secondary Ribs

Insert the secondary ribs into the weaving, just hiding the points under the first available weaver (these do not reach all the way into the ear as did the primary ribs).

Following is a suggested placement for the secondary ribs. If you find they fit better in other places, place them where they fit best.

Place #1s under #1 primary
Place #2s under #2 primary
Place #3s under #4 primary
Place #4s under #5 primary

See **Diagram 26** for placement of all secondary ribs.

Finishing The Basket

Because of the shape of this basket, there will be an area on the corners that does not fill in evenly. After you add all the secondary ribs, resume weaving, going over and under all the ribs and the hoops. Continue until the weaving reaches the point that the ribs begin their corner curve. At this point, stop weaving. Start a new weaver at the center of the rim at the end of the basket. See **Diagram 27**.

After soaking, fold the new, long weaver in half, wrap it around the rim hoop and weave with one end at a time. Place a clothespin on the weaver at the rim to hold it in place. Begin weaving over and under as usual with one end, using more clothespins to position the weaver and ribs as you continue to the other rim and reverse. You will be weaving now from the center, outward. When the first end of the weaver is all woven, begin weaving with the other end, alternating the "overs and unders." Continue by adding new weavers to both ends, until the center weaving reaches the corners. See **Diagram 28**.

Squeeze weavers in around the rim as long as there is any room. When you can no longer squeeze another weaver in, turn around the first rib, reversing just as you did around the rim. The filling in is just like that on an Egg basket; it just happens that the space to be filled in on this basket is at the corners.

NOTE: Occasionally, all the weaving works out evenly and no filling in is necessary, especially if you make a concerted effort to "squeeze" weavers tightly together.

NOTE: The directions given here will produce a 10" square ribbed basket. There are also 6" x 6", 8" x 8", and 12" x 12" square hoops available. Following are the rib lengths for the other 3 sizes:

6" x 6" SQUARE

Rib #1 - 11½"   Rib #3 - 12½"
Rib #2 - 10½"   Rib #4 - 12"
Rib #5 - 10½"

8" x 8" SQUARE **

Rib #1 - 14½"   Rib #3 - 16½"
Rib #2 - 15½"   Rib #4 - 16"
Rib #5 - 14½"

12" x 12" SQUARE

Rib #1 - 22¼"   Rib #3 - 24½"
Rib #2 - 23½"   Rib #4 - 23½"
Rib #5 - 21"

SECONDARY RIBS

Rib #S1 - 21"   Rib #S3 - 23"
Rib #S2 - 22½"   Rib #S4 - 20"
Rib #S5 - 19½"

** Cut four more ribs (two for each side) 16½" long and trim them to fit.

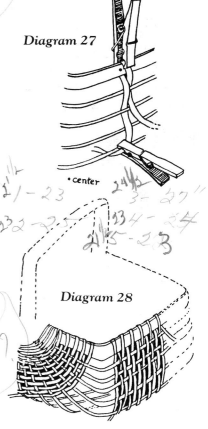

Diagram 27

Diagram 28

BIBLIOGRAPHY

Bennett, Jim. *Handling White Oak*, 1985. Deer Track Crafts, 8215 Beeman Rd., Chelsea, MI 48118.

Boy Scouts of America. *Basketry*, 1968. Boy Scouts of America, Supply Division, Midwestern Distribution Center, 1930 N. Mannheim Rd., Melrose Park, IL 60160.

Burr, Marion Sober. *Basket Patterns*, 1975. Marion Sober Burr, Box 294, Plymouth, MI 48170.

Cary, Mara. *Basic Baskets*, 1975. Boston: Houghton Mifflin.

Christopher, F.J. *Basketry*, 1952. New York: Dover Publishing Co. Inc.

Eaton, Allen H. *Handicrafts Of The Southern Highlands*, 1973. New York: Dover Publications Inc.

Hart, Carol and Dan. *Natural Basketry*, 1976. New York: Watson-Guptill Publications.

Horowitz, Elinor L. *Mountain People, Mountain Crafts*, 1974. New York: J.P. Lippincott Co.

Irwin, John Rice. *Baskets And Basketmakers In Southern Appalachia*, 1982. Schiffer Publishing Co., Box E, Exton, PA 19341.

Jacobs, Betty E.M. *Growing Herbs And Plants For Dyeing*, 1977. Select Books, Route 1, Box 129C, Mountain View, MO 65548.

Johnson, Kay. *Canework*, 1986. London: Dryad Press Ltd.

La Plantz, Shereen. *Plaited Basketry: The Woven Form*, 1982. Press de La Plantz, 899 Bayside Cutoff, Bayside, CA 95524.

Larason, Lew. *The Basket Collectors Book*, 1978. Scorpio Publications, 2 E. Butler Street, Chalfont, PA 18914.

Lasansky, Jeanette. *Willow, Oak and Rye*, 1979. Keystone Books, Pennsylvania State University Press, 215 Wagner Building, University Park, PA 16802.

Pulleyn, Rob. *The Basketmakers Art*, 1987. Lark Books, 50 College Street, Asheville, NC 28801.

Schiffer, Nancy. *Baskets*, 1984. Schiffer Publishing Ltd., Box E, Exton, PA 19341.

Stephenson, Sue M. *Basketry Of The Appalachian Mountains*, 1977. New York: Van Nostrand Reinhold Co.

Teleki, Gloria Roth. *The Baskets Of Rural America*, 1975. New York: E.P. Dutton and Co.

Teleki, Gloria Roth. *Collecting Traditional Basketry*, 1979. New York: E.P. Dutton and Co.

Thompson, Frances. *Antique Baskets And Basketry*, 1985. Wallace-Homestead Book Co., 580 Waters Edge, Lombard, IL 60148.

Thompson, Frances. *Wallace-Homestead Price Guide To Baskets*, 1987. Wallace-Homestead Book Co., 580 Waters Edge, Lombard, IL 60148.

Tod, Osma Gallinger. *Earth Basketry*, 1972. New York: Crown Publishers.

Wright, Dorothy. *The Complete Book Of Baskets And Basketry*, 1983. N. Pomfret, Vermont: David and Charles, Inc.

MAGAZINES AND NEWSLETTERS

The Basketmakers Quarterly, MKS Publications, Inc., P.O. Box 340, Westland, MI 48135.

Fiberarts, 50 College St., Asheville, NC 28801.

Handwoven, Interweave Press, Inc., 306 N. Washington Ave., Loveland, CO 80537.

The News Basket, 899 Bayside Cutoff, Bayside, CA 95524.

Shuttle, Spindle And Dyepot, Handweavers Guild of America, 65 La Salle Rd., West Hartford, CT 06107.

BASKETMAKERS GUILDS AND ASSOCIATIONS

Association Of Michigan Basketmakers
28 Faculty Way, Bloomfield Hills, MI 48013.
The Basket Weavers Guild Of Florida
10412 Ebbit Rd., Jacksonville, FL 32216.
The Basketweavers Guild Of Georgia
BWGG, Patricia Alexander, P.O. Box 1309, Roswell,
GA 30077.
Bay Area Basketmakers
BABM, Maxine Kirmeyer, P.O. Box 24815, San Jose,
CA 95154.
Cape Cod Basketry Guild
CCBG, Dale Michaels Wade, P.O. Box 810, Orleans,
MA 02653.
High Country Basketry Guild
HCBG, K.C. Seibert, 7712 Gromwell Court,
Springfield, VA 22151.

Iowa Basket Weavers Guild
IBWG, Kathy Kellenberger, RR#1, South Amana,
IA 52334.
Los Angeles Basketry Guild
LABG, Judy Mulford, 2098 Mandeville Canyon Rd.,
Los Angeles, CA 90049.
North Carolina Basketmakers Association
NCBA, Judy Wobbleton, 305 Chanute Rd.,
Goldsboro, NC 27530.
Northeast Basketmakers Guild
NBG, P.O. Box 9144, Bolton, CT 06043.
Houston Area Basket Guild
Lynn Gammon, 14627 Wind Hollow Circle,
Houston, TX 77040.
Northwest Basketmakers Guild
NWBG, P.O. Box 5657, Lynnwood, WA 98036.

SUPPLIERS OF BASKETRY MATERIALS

(All are full line suppliers unless otherwise noted.)

ACP
Rt. 9, Box 301-C
Salisbury, NC 28144

Allen's Basket Works
8624 SE 13th St.
Portland, Or 97202

Alnap Co. Inc.
646 South Road
Poughkeepsie, NY 12601

Bob's Baskets
304 Miltwood Rd.
Greensboro, NC 27408
(Hand-cut dogwood handles and baskets)

Brown Ash Basketry
Box 183
Franconia, NH 03580
("Sweetster" baskets made of brown ash)

Cane And Basket Supply
1283 Cochran Ave.
Los Angeles, CA 90019

The Caning Shop
926 Gilman St.
Berkeley, CA 94710

Carol's Canery
Rt. 1, Box 48
Palmyra, VA 22963

Connecticut Cane And Reed
P.O. Box 1276
Manchester, CT 06040
(wonderful selection of books)

Crooked River Crafts, Inc.
P.O. Box 917
La Farge, WI 54639
(colored reed and dyes)

The Country Seat
Box 24, RD 2
Kempton, PA 19529

Earth Guild
One Tingle Alley
Asheville, NC 28801

Frank's Cane And Basketry Supply
7244 Heil Ave.
Huntington Beach, CA 92647

Plymouth Cane And Reed
1170 W. Ann Arbor Rd.
Plymouth, MI 48178

Royalwood Ltd.
517 Woodville Rd.
Mansfield, OH 44907

Sarah's Basket
Rt. 2, Box 22-C
Fayetteville, NC 28382

The Canery
224 S. Liberty St. Annex
Winston Salem, NC 27101

W.A.G.E. Enterprises
Rt. 11, Box 366-A
Goldsboro, NC 27530

INDEX

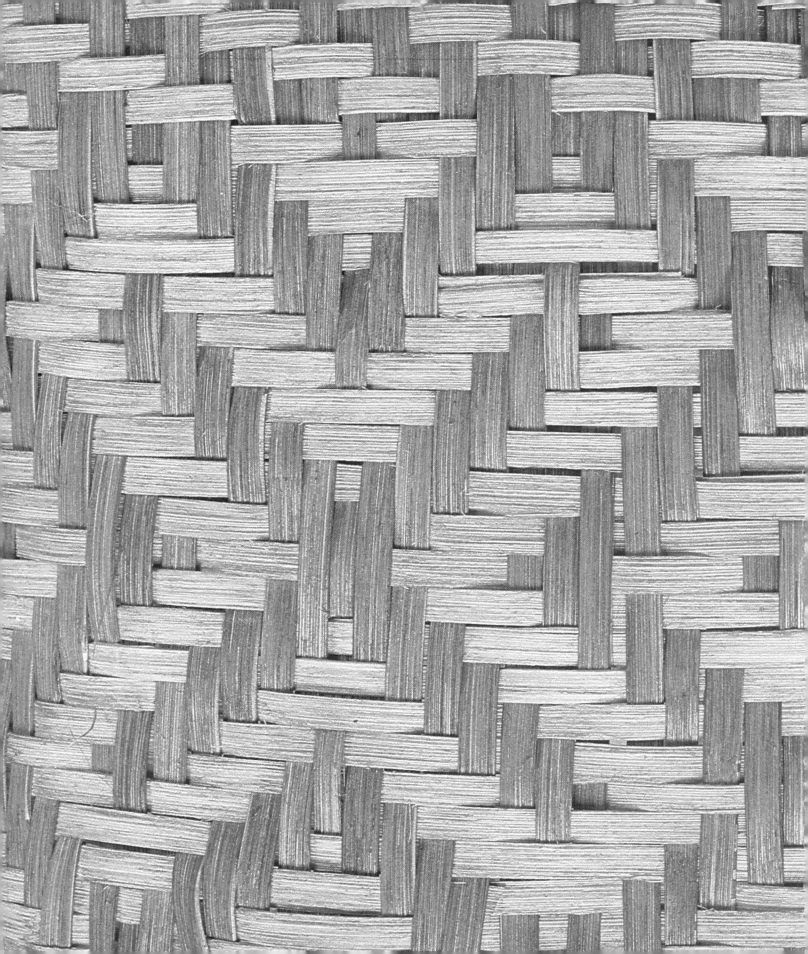